hello

keto

COOKBOOK

JACQUELINE WHITEHART

Pepik Books

York

www.helloketocookbook.com

Text © Jacqueline Whitehart 2019

Jacqueline Whitehart asserts her moral right to be

identified as the author of this work.

A catalogue record for this book is

available from the British Library.

ISBN: 978-0-9955318-7-1

4

YOUR 1-2-3 BEGINNER'S GUIDE TO KETO

INTRODUCTION FROM JAC

Hello!

I'm a 44-year old Mum of three, living and working in York, England.

My journey with Keto started just 6 months ago...

For years and years, I've been watching my figure. Denying myself treats and luxuries. Exercising a lot. Thinking about, maybe even obsessing about food.

And to be honest, it's not done any good. My weight has crept up and up, especially since I turned the big 4-0.

I remember, back when I was in my early 30s, and after the birth of my first child. I thought, "time to shift this baby weight", so I watched what I ate and ate low fat foods. I even went to the gym once or twice. And the weight just went.

I was one of those people that would say, "all you need to do to lose weight is to eat less and move more."

Well let me tell you I am not one of those people anymore!

Since I've hit my 40s, literally nothing has worked. I've exercised daily - just made me eat more. I've fasted - made me hangry and miserable. I've cut back on snacks and treats – had a negative effect.

Let me explain a bit more about snacks and treats. Like many people I find it hard to resist the lure of the fridge, the biscuit tin and a glass of wine. And to be truthful, if I could avoid snacking, I know I would be, if not losing weight, at least maintaining it. Instead I am slowly and surely gaining weight. But I've never been able to avoid snacking. It's not about will-power. It's about tiredness, hormones... but most importantly it's about the rollercoaster of food denial and hunger. The over-eating that comes at the end of a hard day when I say, "stuff it".

If any of this rings true for you then read on...

The psychology of "eating less and moving more" works great for younger people – I see my 15-year old just burning calories as she talks nineteen to the dozen. But as you get older, it works less and less. The signals for hunger and cravings get stronger. You can't, for example, do a high impact spinning class, without getting really hungry afterwards. And to put it bluntly our bodies are less efficient at processing the food, and much more inclined to store the calories as fat. In the time of our ancestors, we'd already be at our life expectancy so it's almost as if our bodies have given up.

Of course, the modern lifestyle of processed foods and an over-abundance of sugar doesn't help either. And the older we get, the longer we have been exposed to these foods and have been "eating for convenience".

Yet, even as I struggled on, depriving myself and "eating healthily", I still didn't want to embrace Keto for a long time.

Why? I'm not totally sure anymore. But I think it was to do with the reputation, the stigma of Keto. It's all a bit 'faddy' isn't it? My facebook is full of scary miracle "keto cures". Is it just me who gets Facebook ads with bowls of what looks like frogspawn and "she ate this every night before bed..."?

It is totally true that the internet has been taken over with mad "keto cures" that strive to rid you of your money. In fact, you can't do a web search for keto without being assaulted by craziness. The real genuine people are there, but they're hidden behind a web of dangerous advertising.

Even now, even though I can see myself losing weight (and feeling full of strength and energy) and KNOW that it is working for me, I still feel a bit of a fraud. Am I turning into one of those keto gurus, selling magical cures to the masses? I sincerely hope not.

The reason behind this book is simple. I wanted a book for someone like me. The book I couldn't find myself. I am not a purveyor of miracles. I am not a twenty-something instagram bunny, oozing keto perfection out of every pore. I'm just an ordinary woman, wanting to share what works for me.

Jacqueline

Jac Whitehart, Founder Jac's Healthy Recipes

Facebook & Instagram: jacshealthyrecipes

WHY HAVE TRADITIONAL DIETS STOPPED WORKING?

Do you feel that you are going backwards in your healthy journey? Do you have to fight for each pound lost? And then you put the weight back on with one nice meal?

Are you finding it easier to gain weight and MUCH harder to lose it?

This book is for anyone who has struggled to lose weight by traditional diets and by "calories in, calories out".

As you get older, your natural metabolism slows down, meaning it gets harder for your body to convert food into energy and easier for it to turn food into body fat. This process normally begins at some time in our early 40s and carries on for the rest of our lives. As with wrinkles, this is a natural part of aging, and there's very little we can do about it – we just have to work a little bit harder.

Three things happen as we age, that makes us actively gain weight:

1   Our ability to convert calories to energy starts to decline

2   Hormonal changes affect our sleep quality, which in turn leads to more food cravings and less ability to resist temptation

3   Our digestive systems and gut
bacteria change and are less able
to process food properly

Sadly, the first two things we can't do much about, but we can lessen the impact on our digestive systems by upping our fibre content (very important for anyone following a keto program) and by adding 'live foods' to our diet. I'm a big fan of kefir and also kombucha.

IS KETO THE ANSWER?

Only you can decide if Keto is something that will work for you. I think that for anyone who has struggled to lose weight through conventional methods, then it is definitely worth considering.

Let's start with a bit of myth-busting. The good, the bad and the ugly of keto.

Keto is very very simply about restricting carbs in your diet. Keto is short for ketosis, which is a chemical function of our bodies where we burn fat for energy instead of carbs. To reach ketosis, you need to eat 40g (or less) of carbs per day. You don't need to be constantly in ketosis to lose weight.

The second part of keto is to eat wholesome foods – that means no processed foods or sugars.

There's a fascinating, controversial and well-regarded film about the Keto diet, called "The Magic Pill". At the time of writing it is available on Netflix (or just find it on youtube). Even if you choose not to believe everything it says, it's arguments are very compelling. My take on it is that there is a lot more research to be done on keto as a health cure. At the same time, I am reassured that keto is safe and very effective for weight loss.

You'll be glad to know that I'm not an extreme keto follower. I follow a really practical plan, that involves *Active Keto* for up to 12 weeks. After that, it's not about the keto diet, it's about a change to a healthier lifestyle - but one that involves carbs and occasional treats.

Luckily, the food industry is embracing the science of keto and allowing us many more options to buy keto-friendly food. On the other hand, we are being bombarded with processed rubbish to buy all the time - weird, huh?

I can honestly say, hand on heart, that one of the biggest changes in my personal psychology is that I'm not tempted by these treats. There's a snack table in the office where I work. It's often piled high with the multi-packs of biscuits or cakes. Everyone in the office has a "cake day". A once a year treat to celebrate when they joined the company. But there's 20+ people in the office so you can imagine how often that table is laden with cakes that we are encouraged to "eat up or else they will go to waste."

This has been the bane of my life for many years. After a healthy lunch, I was unable to resist grazing at the snack table for something to go with my cup of tea. I have a very sweet tooth and would be totally unable to walk away. I still have a sweet tooth and I make delicious treats for me with natural sweeteners to fill that gap (don't worry I'll be showing you *exactly* how to make them yourself). Now

I can see that snack table for what it is and avoid it. What's even more important is that I'm avoiding it happily. I'm not dragging myself away making myself miserable, it just doesn't call to me like it used to. This is how keto has helped me.

KETO SEEMS TOO RADICAL...

I do totally understand if you're worried by some of the things you've read about Keto. Maybe you think it's too great a lifestyle change? Maybe you are worried that you'll never eat bread again. Or maybe you're like Nadia, who asked me:

"I assume Keto means no alcohol? Ever?"

Let me try and put your mind at ease about my own approach to keto. It's just not that crazy...

First of all, to be in a state of ketosis you do need to be eating virtually no carbs - that means no bread and no alcohol.

But to lose weight on a low carb lifestyle **you don't need to be in ketosis all the time**. What you need is to have a significant phase of keto - that's at least 3 days - to reach the weight-loss zone. How long you stay in that zone is up to you. So if you go out for a special meal and want to eat carbs you can. You'll leave ketosis and it will take you 2-3 days to get back to ketosis afterwards but it won't be the end of the world.

The first time you try to reach the keto state is the hardest (lack of energy, possible carb flu - don't worry I'll talk you through these in detail) but I cycle in and out of ketosis all the time and I hardly notice it.

A PERSONAL APPROACH

Let me talk you through my very personal approach to Keto:

STAGE 1 – FIRE UP KETO

This stage lasts for a week and gets all the hard bits out of the way. It's the phase where you go from lots of carbs to no carbs all in one week. It is probably the toughest part of keto. If you can do this, you can do anything. And I'll talk you through it step by step with all the help and tips I can offer.

STAGE 2 - ACTIVE KETO

Once you're in the zone, there's a few tweaks you can make to really get your weight-loss going. I only suggest you follow this for up to 12 weeks. This is the weight-loss zone where you can lose a significant amount of weight.

STAGE 3 - LOW CARB AND SUGAR FREE LIFESTYLE

I truly believe that keto isn't forever. It's a tool to kickstart your weight-loss and inspire your new healthier lifestyle. And what's more, in this phase yes you can have carbs again – but only the good ones – and you can enjoy a glass of wine or two.

STILL NOT SURE YOU WANT TO GET INTO KETO?

Here's 3 things you can do as a gentle introduction to keto...

If these 3 simple changes improve your life (less cravings, less snacks, better sleep) then this is a possible signal that a Keto lifestyle will be a good fit for you.

1 MCT OIL

MCT oil is a food supplement that reduces hunger and cravings. It also makes you reach a state of ketosis quicker and with slightly more carbs.

Go to www.helloketocookbook.com/ to find my recommended links for purchase

2 INULIN

Inulin is a natural prebiotic fibre that aids digestion and most importantly improves sleep quality. I take half a teaspoon in a cup of peppermint tea (any bedtime drink is fine – although obviously avoid caffeine) about half an hour before bed.

Go to www.helloketocookbook.com/ to find my recommended links for purchase.

3 REDUCE YOUR CARBS WHERE POSSIBLE BUT

DON'T ELIMINATE...

For example, pick a salad instead of a sandwich. Whether you are feeding the family or just yourself, it's easy to not put the carb portion on your plate. If you're having a curry, skip the rice. Or avoid the potatoes and have an extra portion of vegetables. It may seem hard at first but you'll soon get used to it and not be tempted by the carbs.

If you notice small improvements that could be a sign that following keto will have a positive impact for you.

By starting with just a teaspoon or two of MCT oil a day, you should notice that cravings between meals will reduce. This should lead to a reduction in snacking and make you feel more in control.

Having half a tsp of inulin stirred into a cup of your favourite bedtime drink should improve sleep quality, which will in turn lessen your cravings and calorie consumption the next day. Sleep deprivation is one of the key problems that lead to weight gain.

Reducing your carbs won't give you the full keto experience and probably won't lead to weight loss directly, but you will probably find that you are less reliant on carbs than you think. You may also have more energy and improved digestion.

THE SCIENCE BEHIND KETO

This book is not a scientific guide to keto, it's very much a personal and practical approach.

However, I feel it's really important to take a quick look at the science – it's so different to all the other "calories in, calories out" diets. It really fascinates me. It has helped me get to grips with the fact that our modern diet may be at fault for our carb-laden approach to food.

"A ketogenic (keto) diet is a low carb, higher fat diet that helps you lose weight and boosts your energy levels."

Ketosis is when your body burns fat for energy instead of carbohydrates. Ketosis is a completely normal metabolic function. When your body doesn't have enough carbohydrates for energy, it will burn stored fat instead.

What are ketones / ketosis?

Ketones are hormones produced by the liver. When you restrict carbs, this triggers the release of more ketones into the blood. Your muscles and other tissues can then use them for fuel. Removing carbs from your body will cause your body to produce more ketones. When you have enough ketones, your body will switch to getting its fuel from carbs to fat.

Ketones are made in your liver from fatty acids found in food or your own body fat. Therefore, your actually burns fat to make ketones. Ketones are used for energy in lieu of carbs.

The Balance Between Ketones and Insulin

Ketones and insulin are forever tied together. When one goes up, the other goes down. And vice versa. Insulin is released whenever we eat carbohydrates. It allows the glucose from the carbohydrates to be released into the bloodstream as fuel. Carbohydrates are the body's preferred source of fuel, so we need to restrict carbs to allow ketosis to happen.

Removing blood sugar spikes

A ketogenic diet allows the body to maintain glucose levels at a low but healthy level. If you stick to a very small number of carbs per day, glucose levels remain low. This will make it much simpler to eat to satisfy your hunger not your cravings.

The effect of sweeteners on cravings

When you start following a keto plan, sweeteners can be something of a false friend. If you eat something sweet and delicious, your body is going to expect some sugar energy. Your body gets ready to receive the sugar by releasing insulin. But the sweetener cannot be turned into energy as the body expects (it has been fooled!) so your body craves more sugar and the sugar cycle is not broken.

For this reason, in Phase 1 (Fire Up Keto), we remove all sugar and sweeteners and break the cycle. After this stage, food with sweeteners can be re-introduced in small quantities – after all, natural sweeteners are completely keto friendly. It's just about changing food attitudes and getting off the rollercoaster.

How Do you Lose Weight On Keto?

When your body is in ketosis it becomes extremely efficient at burning fat. Following a keto diet forces your body to use up fat stores, making you lose weight.

Ketones are made in your liver from fatty acids. The fatty acids come from both the food that you eat AND your own body fat. When you are in ketosis you are always burning away slowly at your fat stores.

Additionally, if you eat more fat than your body needs, this is not converted into stored body fat (only carbs do this!)

Does MCT Oil Help?

MCT oil is a natural healthy fat. It converts to ketones more easily than other fats. It simply boosts the levels of ketones in your body. If you are just starting out, you reach a state of ketosis quicker and this helps to reduce side effects of the switch. If you are already in ketosis, it naturally reduces hunger and helps you burn fat more efficiently.

It also is the most effective thing I've found at curbing your hunger. You will eat less at meals and be less prone to snacking.

There are various types of MCT oil, but I would highly recommend buying a more premium brand that is pure MCT 8. MCT 8 is the most easily absorbed fat and is converted into ketones most efficiently. The cheaper brands tend to be a mix of MCT 6,8 and 10 and are less effective. The brand that I use is from Keto Source.

Adding MCT oil to your keto plan:

- *Reduces snacking*
- *Increases fat burning*
- *Help you reach ketosis quicker*
- *Limits 'keto flu' symptoms*

It does not curb carb cravings, but ketosis does. You need to wait until you have been in ketosis for at least a few days for carb cravings to disappear.

WHY IS MY APPROACH DIFFERENT?

And How Is It Going To Work For You?

Every single approach to dieting I see, whether it's Keto, low calorie or fasting, fails to take into account the ups and downs of everyday life. It fails to allow for the hormones, the chocolate cravings, the family dinners, the weddings... these are the richness of our lives and we would be lost and miserable without them.

Time and again, I get emails from people saying they lost weight and then something happened, and they put it back on again. And now they don't know what to do.

Katie says,

> *"I am about to embark on this journey, weight has always been an issue and I have had many failures. In other aspects of my life I have achieved many things through determination and prove people wrong, however when it comes to losing weight this determination seems to leave me and I fail every time. I can lose several pounds and then nothing. No-one can explain why I can't lose the weight."*

Jo says,

> *"I have lost 2 stone in the past using the 5.2 diet, but after breaking my ankle last year I put it all back on."*

I approach this plan in a different way. There are 3 different stages – Stage 1 "Fire Up Keto" is the adjustment stage (it's just a week don't worry), Stage 2 is "Active Keto" and Stage 3 is "Lower Carb lifestyle".

You can follow *Active Keto* for up to 12 weeks. But here's the important bit - you can dip in and out of Stage 2. You can swap to Stage 3 whenever you want or need. Stage 3 allows for good carbs, a glass or two of wine and generally a bit of indulgence. And allows you to hop back on the *Active Keto* wagon when you're ready.

What's really important is that Keto is not about deprivation – you don't get that crushing hunger and light-headedness that is crucial to low calorie weight-loss. What's more, by adapting it to your lifestyle and giving yourself a "keto holiday" now and again, it's a plan that tries to break the 'rollercoaster' of dieting and eliminates the guilt.

Still Worried About Giving Up Bread & The Sweet Stuff?

I understand because I remember this feeling well. I'm dreadful for wanting something sweet after a meal. And that's why I've got some important recipes for both bread and sweet treats that you can have at any time. I love to have a handful of my delicious chocolates after my dinner. I feel satiated at last. And I adore my seed bread toast - it's a dark bread in the style of a rye bread. It's so satisfying. And you can keep it in the freezer and toast a slice whenever you want.

If you look up keto on the internet, there's a lot of obsessives out there. Telling you all these crazy things to eat. Constantly telling you how to cut out a gram of carbs here and a gram there. That's no way to live!

So here's how it's going to work. We're going to cut back the carbs from the hundreds of grams you currently eat to about 40g a day. But we're not going to count carbs! We're just going to follow a few simple rules. If you embrace one of the meal plans or just make sure you don't stray from the rules then you can easily hit the 40g target.

What About Dairy?

Many keto plans are very meat-orientated and ban dairy. The science behind this is unclear. I think many people have dairy intolerances (including some very influential keto-ers) and many keto followers have hopped on this band wagon.

There's dairy in my plan. I think it's an essential source of fats and protein for vegetarians. There's a huge variety of flavours in cheese and can make or break a meal. I also love Greek Yogurt, which is about as low carb as dairy can get (about 3g per portion), and I sometimes use to indulge my sweet tooth. A generous portion of Greek yogurt, a few drops of vanilla paste and a little sweetener - yum yum!

But if you are dairy free (but not vegetarian) then there's plenty of options for you too.

Vegetarian & Vegan

The first thing to note is that "traditional keto" is incredibly meat heavy. If you watch "The Magic Pill", you'll see that one family end up buying a cow! I think in the UK, we traditionally eat less red meat than Americans, from where the Keto diet originated.

What do you eat on keto if you don't eat meat? Meat is a great source of protein and fats and it's great to fill your plate with a huge steak and lots of veggies. It's just not what I want.

In *The Hello Keto* plan, there is quite a lot of meat but also plenty of alternatives, often with a dairy or egg component to give you the protein and fats that you need.

The problem comes for vegans, where a lot of protein sources - beans, pulses etc - also contain carbohydrates. Too many carbohydrates to reach ketosis unfortunately.

As a vegan can't easily follow *Active Keto*, I recommend the Hello Keto plan for vegetarians but not for vegans.

(If you're a vegan reading this, then don't totally despair. There's plenty of recipes that are vegan and you will find The Lower Carb Lifestyle - which allows beans and pulses - to be a perfect route to a healthier diet)

Our perfect state for optimum and lasting weight-loss is Mild ketosis, which we can reach comfortably on this plan in both Stage 1 and Stage 2. Over the next few chapters, I will 'hold your hand' and guide you through exactly what you need to do to reach mild ketosis and embrace this new style of living.

STAGE 1: FIRE UP KETO

ONE WEEK TO START YOUR KETO JOURNEY

You've decided that it's time to try Keto. Great!

Finding Your Keto Mindset

I understand that you're a little anxious. It's a lot of changes all at once. You're worried about how you might feel, whether you'll be hungry. And that underlying niggly fear that you just won't get enough to eat.

Remember that there are two parts to keto, the first to reduce carbs is known to everyone. But the second, to eliminate processed foods is actually harder to get your head around. In the first week, you might end up doing a bit more food preparation than normal. But don't worry, there's actually plenty of pre-made fresh and non-processed foods you can buy if you're short of time.

Are We Going To Count Carbs?

Yes and no!

We are going to restrict carbs in the first week to about 40g carbs per day. But the good news is I'm going to do the carb counting for you and give you a plan to follow that will mean you are restricting your carbs without having to think about it too much. You can follow the meal plan exactly or mix and match with other recipes from this book – they're all low carb so feel free to experiment.

Rule for Fire Up: Keep Daily Carbs below 40g

For the first week, I'm going to hold your hand right the way through. I'll give you a completely structured plan that you can follow to the letter. There's a dedicated Meal Plan, shopping list, coping strategies and answers to all your questions.

Preparation

I advise that you prepare a little before you start, make sure you have the right foods in the house and know your options when you're out and about.

Before you begin, you should check what's in your cupboards and eat up or throw away all the tempting foods.

I hate wasting good food, but that is sometimes my downfall. I can't throw away food that's in date even if I know it's bad for me.

Luckily/unluckily I have many people in my house that are happy to eat up the foods I can't eat. I say unluckily because this means I still have to buy pasta and bread and biscuits and have them lurking round the house. I've found with Keto that I don't go hunting down the sweet stuff at 10pm. In the past I've been known to eat nutella straight from the jar!

Do a clean sweep before you start your first week of keto. If you have family or a partner to feed, keep food that's just for them. But if there is food/leftovers that they don't like or won't eat, then make sure you dispose of that before you start.

Don't worry too much, when you get through the first week, I promise those cravings will go away so you won't need to worry too much.

Remember the biggest difference between Keto and EVERY OTHER DIET is that doing Keto you never feel deprived or hungry AND cravings are substantially reduced. That's why it works so well, willpower and the traditional diet rollercoaster will no longer apply to you... isn't that wonderful?

Before we get started on your meal plans and shopping list for the first week, I want to introduce you to a few things that you might want to stock up on to help you as you transition to keto.

For a lot of people, myself very much included, the hardest things to give up are bread and chocolate. That's why in this book, I'm giving you detailed instructions on how to make your own sugar free and ultra-low carb versions.

But I don't want you to feel overwhelmed at this stage of the plan. You are welcome to skip ahead and look at the recipes for bread (chocolate we have to leave until *Active Keto*) and if you want to try one of the bread recipes go right ahead.

WHAT TO EAT ON A KETO DIET?

Before we get onto the recipes and meals you can eat let's just make a list of foods you can eat as much as you want of (no or ultra-low carbs), foods that you can eat in moderation (low carb) and foods to avoid (too many carbs).

Eat As Much As You Want

Chicken
All fish and shellfish
Red meat such as beef, lamb etc
Cheese – all varieties except 'low fat'
Eggs
Green vegetables
Cauliflower
Aubergine
Onion and garlic
Herbs, spices and stock
Nuts and seeds
Almond milk
Coconut including coconut milk

Foods To Eat In Moderation

(as a rough guide no more than 2 portions of these foods every day)

Red, yellow and orange vegetables
Tomatoes, including tinned tomatoes

Red and black berries – strawberries (yes I know that officially this is not a berry!), blueberries, raspberries, blackberries, red and blackcurrants

Greek yogurt

Milk in small quantities (eg. in a cup of tea)

Foods To Avoid

Bread

Pasta

Rice

Potatoes

Sugar – includes cakes, biscuits, chocolate

Sweet potatoes

Squashes – butternut, pumpkin etc

Beans – kidney beans, butter beans, haricot beans etc

Pulses – lentils and chickpeas

For some of these, bread, sweet treats etc, I'll introduce you to substitutes. They're not quite the same but you'll learn to love them...

And for the last four things on the list – sweet potato, the squash family, beans and pulses – I have good news. We'll be reintroducing them when the *Active Keto* phase is over, and we move towards a sugar free lifestyle.

Although all green veggies are allowed on keto, they do contain a small amount of carbohydrate. Here are the best veggies (where you really can go wild!)

Low Carb Veggies

less than 3% carbs

- *Celery*
- *lettuce and salad leaves*
- *spinach*
- *cucumber*
- *kale*
- *avocado*
- *tomatoes*
- *asparagus*
- *broccoli*
- *cabbage*
- *cauliflower*
- *mushrooms*
- *pak choi*

A Typical 'Fire Up' Keto Day

A light breakfast

A hearty salad with plenty of meat or cheese

OR

A warming soup with a slice of low carb bread

A big dinner – perhaps a Soul Food Bowl

OR

*Simply tasty chicken with
lots and lots of veggies*

First Week Snacking

It's important to realise that you can and should snack *WHENEVER YOU WANT* during the 'Fire Up' Phase.

The snacks that you have during this phase must be (a) carb free and (b) unsweetened.

You can't have sugar or sweeteners during this week. I'll explain a little bit more about why we avoid sweetened food during this phase in 'The Sugar Rollercoaster'.

My Top 3 'Fire Up' Keto Snacks (Have These Available Always!)

For a simpler kickstart to Keto, here are my top 3 things to always have in stock when I'm feeling peckish:

1 BABYBEL CHEESE

Babybel is a natural (non-processed) cheese consisting of just 3 ingredients - milk, salt and natural enzymes. It's mild taste and flavour coupled with its convenience make it a great choice when you're in need of a snack. I often have one (or two) mid-afternoon when I come back from picking up the kids from school. It just fills that gap nicely.

2 SALTED PEANUTS

Peanuts are probably not part of your current diet - because they are high in fat you have learnt to avoid them as "bad for you". But I can tell you that they are absolutely allowed and make a really tasty snack. Salted peanuts contain just 3 ingredients - peanuts, salt and oil. I like KP nuts as they are very low carb - just 1.7g per 30g portion.

3 OLIVES

Olives are rich in healthy fats, very natural and tasty. Because of their natural high mono-unsaturated fat content, they are very filling and can help fill a gap. I like to buy a mix of interesting flavours or stuffed olives for variety. Olives are more flavoursome if warmed to room temperature before eating.

THE SUGAR ROLLERCOASTER

The first week of keto can be tricky – especially if you eat a lot of sugary carb-laden foods. When you deprive your body of carbohydrates, the first thing your body is likely to do is panic!

This is why during the first week, we follow a strict meal plan and only allow savoury snacks.

The psychology behind this is simple. When you first start the plan, your motivation is high, but your body is weak. You might well get cravings for sugary things and alcohol. For one week only, you have to say 'NO'. Knowing that we will be introducing sweet treats in the following week means that you only have to get through one week...

Sugar and sweeteners are an interesting problem. Unlike starchy carbs (bread, rice etc) which you might miss as bulk to a meal but can be relatively easily substituted, you can get real problems with cravings for sugar and sweet foods. If you choose to use sweeteners and make low carb treats you are satisfying that craving but you are not getting to the root of the problem.

The goal of *Fire Up Week* is to dramatically cut your sugar cravings, stop your insulin spiking and heal your unhealthy relationship to the sweet stuff. All of that in one week of avoiding sweet treats. Pretty cool huh? Even better, when you allow yourself to go back to occasional chocolate and puddings in *Active Keto*, you'll find yourself naturally wanting less and needing less sweetness.

Understanding The Difference Between Hunger & Cravings

To help you get through this first week, it's really important to understand the difference between hunger and cravings. Hunger makes you feel weak, makes your tummy rumble and can make you rather grumpy! We're not going to go hungry during *Fire Up Keto*. You'll eat 3 meals a day and if you're hungry you just have a snack.

For example, I might start with a keto shake, have an avocado and egg salad for lunch and have a soul food bowl for dinner. But come mid-afternoon (I get home at about 4pm after doing the school run and there's still hours before dinner) I'll be hungry and in need of a snack. Babybel and a generous handful of peanuts really hit the spot at that time for me. What's your 'hungry time'? What ideas do you have to combat it? Having a plan in place really helps you overcome any temptations.

Cravings are something completely different. You're not actually hungry, you don't feel weak and wobbly. But you have an irrational need for something, something sweet. My weakness is after a meal. After lunch or dinner, I want something sweet to finish it off. This is entirely psychological. My body has become used to a sweet course, but it doesn't need it.

As a side note, I realised I was doing this to my children as well. I'd always offer them yogurt and fruit followed by a biscuit with their dinner. Now I just offer them yogurt and fruit and skip the biscuit. There's been only limited resistance. I was building up a pattern of behaviour that would not serve them well for the future.

During Fire Up we are going to 'look those cravings in the eye' and say "No, I'm not hungry it's just a craving." Sometimes it will be hard, but if we crush those cravings this week, we will be setting ourselves up for a lifetime of healthier eating. Whenever you feel those cravings, tell yourself (1) it's just for a week and (2) about the amazing benefits you are getting.

What is "Keto Flu" And How Do You Avoid It?

You may have read about Keto flu in advance of trying the keto plan and you might be worrying about it.

Have you heard tales of slumping energy levels, headaches and digestive upset? I'm going to tell you the honest truth… it's really not that bad!

And also give you some tips to limit any effects.

Keto flu is the name given to the symptoms that you might suffer when you switch from a normal to a keto diet. As you start to restrict carbs, your insulin levels drop, and your body enters a fasting state. This is similar to the state you enter when you fast, but you won't be hungry. The fasting state is necessary to create the switch to fat burning. But the fasting state can cause headaches, dizziness and irritability.

Unlike when you are actually fasting, keto dieters can supplement their diet with the foods, vitamins and minerals to alleviate their symptoms.

Sodium, Potassium And Magnesium

As insulin levels drop, these elements leave your body and you could experience symptoms such as light-headedness, headache, heart palpitations or fatigue.

Add foods rich in these minerals to improve your symptoms.

To increase sodium, try snacking on salty foods like peanut butter or cheese. For potassium and magnesium, up your intake of green leafy vegetables, oily fish or nuts and seeds. Avocado is a particularly rich source of both minerals.

You could also try a vitamin energy drink such as Berocca, as this contains magnesium and B vitamins (which help with energy release) to ease your symptoms.

Fat Levels

If you encounter hunger, cravings, irritability, nausea, diarrhoea or fatigue these can be caused by not eating enough fat. When you feel hunger or fatigue, keep snacking on higher fat snacks to ease the symptoms. It will feel weird after a lifetime of "low fat" but it will ease the switch. And remember fat on its own is never "bad", it is a combination of fat and carbs (in 90% of a normal diet and in 99.9% of processed foods) that lead to weight gain.

Digestive Upset

You are going to be radically changing what you eat. At the start your digestive system doesn't really know what to do with itself. You might find your regular bowel movements change; you might be constipated or feel bloated and windy. Although this can feel uncomfortable and unpleasant, know that when you are fully keto-adjusted these problems will disappear and in fact you will have fewer digestive problems than before.

I have found that there is one easy food you can add to your diet (whether you are on keto or not) and your gut will feel so much better. That food is kefir, a fermented milk drink that you can get in every supermarket. Kefir has a few grams of carbs (4-6g per 100g) but just a small amount of kefir gives you all the benefits without damaging your keto program.

I recommend that you look for a natural unsweetened kefir and take about 50ml at a time. You can have your kefir any time of day, but a great time to try it is first thing in the morning, before or with your breakfast. If you feel pain or uncomfortable-ness later on in the day, it is ok to add another 50ml shot of kefir as that should help to settle you.

How To Take MCT Oil During Fire Up Keto

If you are experimenting with MCT oil during *Fire Up Keto*, then this will really help any "keto flu" symptoms. Essentially, MCT will make your switch to keto quicker and easier.

Unfortunately, too much MCT added to your diet too quickly can upset your digestion. We start slow during the first week.

The safest way to start with MCT oil is 1 tsp once or twice a day for the first week, 2 tsp once or twice a day for the second week and 3 tsp (1 tbsp) once or twice a day from the third week onwards.

If you are taking one teaspoon a day (recommended for at least the first 3 days) then the optimal time to take your MCT oil is an hour before lunch.

You should always take MCT oil before a meal (preferably at least half an hour) as this allows time for your ketone levels to rise which will help with hunger and limit what you eat.

If you are taking two separate teaspoons a day (days 4-7 of Fire Up Keto), then the first should be first thing in the morning (preferably about an hour before breakfast) and the second an hour before lunch.

THE AMAZING BENEFITS OF THE FIRE UP WEEK

If you are ever struggling during this first week come back here and look at the benefits you are getting for just one week of hard work.

Got the after-lunch wobbles? Has someone offered you a piece of cake? Desperate for a glass of wine?

Hold this in your head and feel strong:

"I am doing this for me. I want to change my attitude to food. I want to feel healthier and lose weight. To do this I need to be strong for just one week.

I CAN DO THIS…"

And if you follow my advice, get your body into ketosis you will be a fat burning machine by the end of this week.

By the end of *Fire Up Keto*, you will:

1 Be in full ketosis

You will be burning fat instead of carbohydrate. Not only that, you'll be burning your existing fat store as well.

2 Have tons of energy

As you have now switched to burning fat, your energy levels increase hugely, and they will stay that way for as long as you stay in ketosis.

3 Have started to lose weight

As soon as your body shifts to fat burning, you will start to lose weight consistently. There may be a small early spike in weight-loss (3-4 pounds in the first week) or you may fall straight into the pattern of consistent weight-loss of 1-2 pounds per week.

4 Have reduced your cravings for sugary foods

All your hard work resisting cravings is starting to pay off. You'll already feel differently towards treats and sugary junk food.

5   Be feeling great

You're well on your way to a healthier lifestyle. The other benefits will start to kick in. As well as increased energy and weight-loss, your skin tone will improve, and your hair will get thicker and glossier.

LET'S GET COOKING

As we are concentrating on limiting the sugar spike during Fire Up Keto, we start by cutting out sugar and sweeteners. Then we need lots of great ideas for subbing out the starchy carbs to make fulfilling meals. This is simpler than you might expect, as there are lots of ingredients out there that make great alternatives to starchy carbs. We'll also use robust flavours like garlic and spices and look at recipes from all round the world, so it never gets boring.

Replacing Starchy Carbs

Bread

If you're a bread fan, you should definitely get started on the bread recipes in this book. There are two basic breads – *Golden Flaxseed Bread* and *Dark Seeded Bread*. Once you've made the basic bread you can either freeze in slices ready to pop in the toaster or convert into simple crispbreads by baking them once sliced. Crispbreads can be stored in an airtight container for up to 5 days.

A fantastically simple bread recipe is for a *2 Minute Microwave Bread Roll* or *Teacake*. The roll or teacake is made in a completely different way, by microwaving for two minutes. It's a fantastically simple recipe that you can easily knock up for breakfast or mid-afternoon snack.

There's also a great recipe for *Tortilla Wraps*. Perfect for serving alongside one of my Soul Food Bowls.

Naked Noodles

Naked noodles, also called shirataki or konjac noodles, are a fantastic addition to your low carb store cupboard. Firstly, they are a natural ingredient made from the konjac root that has been popular in Japan for years. Secondly, and probably most importantly, they taste great. If you follow my instructions, you can use these noodles in loads of dishes, and you won't taste the difference.

Up until recently you could only buy these noodles from Chinese supermarkets but now you can get them with your normal shopping. The brand I like is "Bare naked noodles" as they have a great consistency. I use these to make huge bowls of Ramen noodles, that are so warming and satisfying.

Cooking Naked Noodles

1 Drain the liquid off the noodles first then place in a large bowl or pan. Cover with cold water.

2 Drain the noodles and refresh the water up to 3 times, until any lingering smell has gone.

3 Dry the noodles on kitchen paper.

4 Heat a generous quantity of oil in a large saucepan (at least 1 tsp per person but no need to stint) to a med-high heat. Add the noodles and stir-fry for about 3 minutes.

5 The noodles can then be eaten with a stir-fry or loaded into a ramen.

Cauliflower

Yes, you've probably heard that cauliflower is a great substitute for rice and carbs. But it can end up being disappointing. It's got quite a strong flavour, and this only increases when chopped up small to make cauliflower rice. I go the other way and use small florets and robust spicy flavours to make a delicious dish. I like all-in-one dishes with cauliflower and meat, cheese or tofu to make a really satisfying meal.

Cooking At Home Vs Buying Food On The Go

Everyone has a different schedule and different challenges to overcome. I think it's fair to say though that none of us would choose to spend the day slaving over the stove, and for most of us this is nigh on impossible.

Breakfast is probably ok. A bit of preparation at the weekend to make some *Magnificent Muesli* or *Nut and Seed Granola* and you're good for the week.

Dinner is more challenging. But as long as you make sure you buy the ingredients you need in advance; most meals can be rustled up quickly.

But for the majority of us, *lunch* is the real problem. Traditionally, lunch is a quick sandwich or a packed lunch, and is laden with carbs. Go to a café or restaurant and you're stuck for choices too.

Preparation is the key for lunch on-the-go and salad is a good choice. I'm including a whole section of *Lunchbox Meals* that can be packed up and taken to your place of work.

Not got enough time to make a packed lunch? There are also solutions for that too… but be prepared to pay a little bit more.

Top Tips For Keto-Friendly Lunches Out & About

If you're trying very hard to follow a keto plan but can't manage to bring a lunchbox, then it's actually ok to buy something. And luckily, town centre shops and cafes are making it easier for you. If you go to a mini supermarket, M&S or Pret then there are plenty of salad options available and that is what you should head for. M&S food does a huge range of salads with meat, fish or cheese and this is where I normally head if I've forgotten my packed lunch. Look for a salad with no sneaky rice or potatoes and plenty of meat or cheese.

A pre-prepared salad also has the advantage of a separate salad dressing that you should enjoy without guilt.

How To Use Shop-Bought Cooked Meat & Salads To Save You Time

You can buy a plain salad and then add a pack of roasted chicken, mozzarella balls or tofu. You can use this to whizz up a very quick packed lunch salad, just take the dressing separately.

Jac's 2-Minute Salad Option
Choose a combination of items, picking one or two items from each section.

Salad	Protein	Healthy Fats
Salad leaves	Roast ham	Vinaigrette
Baby spinach	Deli meats – chorizo, salami..	Mayonnaise
Cherry tomatoes	Mozzarella balls	Sun-dried tomatoes in oil
	Crumbled Feta	Olives
	Marinated tofu	Nuts
	Spicy Cooked chicken fillets	Seeds
	Smoked or flaked salmon	
	Tinned salmon	
	Tinned tuna	
	Boiled egg	

One final tip for easy lunch heaven – I absolutely love Leon's Garlic Aioli. It will jazz up any salad and is filling and oh so tasty! Amazingly, it's also vegan.

Cooking For Others

I totally understand this conundrum. Following a keto program is that much harder if you have to make separate meals for others who still have carbs in their diet. I get it. I have two teenage girls, one of whom is vegetarian, plus a ten-year-old boy who has "hollow legs" and seems to be constantly hungry. We have to use different tactics on different days. If we're all home together then I'll try and cook something that we can all enjoy together. For example, we all love the Chicken Katsu Curry. I make it with vegetable stock and use seitan in my vegetarian daughter's version. I serve it with a big bowl of white rice that the kids can gorge themselves on. Another family favourite is the Saag Paneer. This one is vegetarian and again I serve with rice and naan breads which I can easily avoid.

There are also plenty of days when we can't all eat together – normally when I'm being "Mum taxi" and am trying to squeeze the kids' dinner into a half hour gap between activities. On these days, I don't feel guilty about feeding them something separately from me. I make them something simple and have one of my "Soul food, bowl food" meals which I always keep stacks of in the freezer!

MEAL PLANS & SHOPPING LIST

There's a Fire Up Meal Plan and a Fire Up Vegetarian Meal Plan. Each is followed by a Shopping List so you can get organised.

Each Meal Plan comes in at under 30g Carbs per day. You can add low carb snacks up to a max of 40g Carbs per day.

You can follow the Meal Plan exactly or feel free to 'Mix & Match' with other recipes that take your fancy.

FIRE UP MEAL PLAN

Monday	Tuesday	Weds	Thursday	Friday	Saturday	Sunday
Chocolate Shake 1.8g carbs (page 109)	Almond Porridge 2.2g carbs (page 112)	Super Veg Smoothie 1.5g carbs (page 111)	Chocolate Shake 1.8g carbs (page 109)	Super Fruit Smoothie 3.8g carbs (page 110)	Big Veggie Breakfast 4.7g carbs (page 117)	Smoked Salmon & Eggs 2.5g carbs (page 119)
Protein Packed Tuna Salad 5.1g carbs (page 124)	Protein Packed Tuna Salad 5.1g carbs (page 124)	Smashed Avocado & Poached Egg 8.1g carbs (page 132)	Greek Lunchbox Salad with Pine Nuts 12.1g carbs (page 126)	Creamy Mushrooms on Toast 5.9g carbs (page 131)	Creamy Mushrooms on Toast 5.9g carbs (page 131)	Easy Bake Goats Cheese Frittata 5.7g carbs (page 123)
Creamy Salmon & Leek Bowl 14.9g carbs (page 160)	Best Beef Chilli 11.3g carbs (page 170)	Best Beef Chilli 11.3g carbs (page 170)	Cod Ramen with Naked Noodles 12g carbs (page 163)	Cod Ramen with Naked Noodles 12g carbs (page 163)	Prawn Thai Fragrant Curry 17.4g carbs (page 157)	Chinese Steak Salad 9.8g carbs (page 149)
22g carbs	18.7g carbs	21.1g carbs	26g carbs	21.8g carbs	28g carbs	18.1g carbs

FIRE UP SHOPPING LIST

FRUIT & VEGETABLES
onion(s) / frozen onions
red onions
shallots
red pepper / frozen peppers
chestnut mushrooms
carrots
broccoli florets
red chillies
beansprouts
leeks
pak choi

cherry tomatoes
salad leaves
spring (green) onions
avocados
baby spinach leaves
fresh coriander
radishes

limes
lemons

DAIRY & EGGS
large eggs
cream cheese
goats cheese
butter
feta
creme fraiche
natural greek yogurt
almond milk

MEAT, CHICKEN & FISH
smoked salmon
salmon fillets
cod fillets
sirloin steak
minced beef 5% fat

HERBS & SPICES
paprika
turmeric
chilli powder
cumin
chilli (red pepper) flakes
dried mixed herbs
dried onion

NUTS & SEEDS
pinenuts
chia seeds
sesame seeds

OIL & VINEGAR
olive oil
balsamic vinegar
white wine vinegar
olive oil
toasted sesame oil
white wine vinegar

STORE CUPBOARD
garlic paste
ginger paste
baking powder
vegetable stock / powder
cocoa powder
1 can coconut milk
2 cans chopped tomatoes
2 cans kidney beans
2 cans tuna
Worcestershire sauce
English mustard
sun-dried tomatoes in oil
white wine

WORLD FOODS
lemongrass paste
palm sugar
fish sauce
mirin
konjac noodles
oyster sauce
soy sauce
light soy sauce
rice vinegar
tomato ketchup

FROZEN
frozen mixed berries
frozen prawns (shrimp)

SPECIALITY
almond flour
erythritol
milled golden flaxseed
psyllium husk powder
protein powder

FIRE UP VEGETARIAN MEAL PLAN

	Monday	Tuesday	Weds	Thursday	Friday	Saturday	Sunday
	Nuts & Seeds Granola 3.3g carbs (page 113)	Nuts & Seeds Granola 3.3g carbs (page 113)	Nuts & Seeds Granola 3.3g carbs (page 113)	Nuts & Seeds Granola 3.3g carbs (page 113)	Nuts & Seeds Granola 3.3g carbs (page 113)	Perfect Pan-cakes 3 Ways 0.8g carbs (page 118)	Perfect Pan-cakes 3 Ways 0.8g carbs (page 118)
	Houmous Stuffed Pepper 11g carbs (page 133)	Creamy Tomato Soup 7.6g carbs (page 138)	Creamy Tomato Soup 7.6g carbs (page 138)	Easy Bake Goats Cheese Frittata 5.7g carbs (page 123)	Easy Bake Goats Cheese Frittata 5.7g carbs (page 123)	Creamy Mushrooms on Toast 5.9g carbs (page 131)	Creamy Mushrooms on Toast 5.9g carbs (page 131)
	Aubergine, Spinach & Paneer Curry 13.6g carbs (page 173)	Cauliflower Tofu Curry 10.8g carbs (page 148)	Cauliflower Tofu Curry 10.8g carbs (page 148)	Aubergine, Spinach & Paneer Curry 13.6g carbs (page 173)	Smashed Avocado & Poached Egg 8.1g carbs (page 132)	Vegetarian Thai Fragrant Curry 22.1g carbs (page 158)	Vegetarian Thai Fragrant Curry 22.1g carbs (page 158)
	27.9g carbs	21.8g carbs	21.8g carbs	22.7g carbs	17.2g carbs	28.8g carbs	28.8g carbs

FIRE UP VEGETARIAN

FRUIT & VEGETABLES
white onion(s) / frozen onions
red onions
red peppers / mixed peppers
green peppers / mixed peppers
cauliflower
chestnut mushrooms
red chillies
babycorn
mange tout
aubergine

tomatoes
cherry tomatoes
spring (green) onions
avocados
baby spinach leaves
fresh coriander leaves

lime(s)
lemons
lime

DAIRY & EGGS
large eggs
cream cheese
goats cheese
paneer cheese
butter
almond milk
double cream
natural greek yogurt
houmous
tofu

HERBS & SPICES
turmeric
cumin
ground coriander
dried mixed herbs
oregano (dried)
garam massala
dried onion
chilli flakes
curry leaves
cumin seeds
mustard seeds
nigella seeds

NUTS & SEEDS
sunflower seeds
pumpkin seeds

chia seeds
macadamia nuts
pecans
chopped mixed nuts
ground almonds

OIL & VINEGAR
balsamic vinegar
white wine vinegar
olive oil
mild olive oil

STORE CUPBOARD
garlic paste
ginger paste
2 cans coconut milk
2 cans chopped tomatoes
tomato paste
white wine
sun-dried tomatoes in oil
vegetarian stock powder
baking powder
vanilla paste

WORLD FOODS
lemongrass paste
palm sugar
fish sauce
soy sauce

SPECIALITY
psyllium husk powder
erythritol
almond flour
milled golden flaxseed
erythritol

MAKING BREAD

Bread is one of the hardest things to make keto-friendly. Wheat flours contain gluten which is important for the rise and texture of the bread.

I'm going to use amazon links to any specialist ingredients so you can source them easily. If you buy through the Amazon link it not only makes it super easy for you, but I also get a small affiliate fee.

In the UK, the brands I favour (for quality "no frills" ingredients) are Real Food Source, Buy Wholefoods Online, Bulk Powders, Sevenhills and NKD Living.

To find the ingredients you need quickly, go to

www.helloketocookbook.com

BREAD ROLLS & TEACAKES

I started playing around with these because I wanted a cheaty way of making low carb bread that you could whip up quickly. I didn't really expect them to be as good as they are!

I often make them for a mid-afternoon snack when I'm feeling peckish. You might even find that you don't need any other bread recipes than these two. Both recipes use a similar combination of ingredients.

The *2-Minute Microwave Bread Roll* is a great option for making a quick sandwich. The *2-Minute Toasted Teacake* is absolutely as good as it sounds. Sweet and cinnamon-y, it gives off a delicious smell when it's being toasted. Spread thickly with butter and you're good to go. (Seriously, I might make myself one right now they're so good!)

The one thing you really need is the right size bowl or cup to cook it in. You need a flat based bowl, cup or large ramekin which is about 10cm/4" diameter at the base. I've got a breakfast bowl that is perfect for the purpose but if you don't have anything suitable I have one listed on

www.helloketocookbook.com

As with some of the other bread recipes you will also need a finely ground almond flour (not ground almonds!) and coconut flour. The brands I use (reasonably priced, good quality and easy to source) are available here:

www.helloketocookbook.com

2 MINUTE BREAD ROLLS

The consistency of this roll is amazing, like real bread.

SERVES	TIME	CARBS	CALS
1	**2 M**	**3.4 G**	**288**

INGREDIENTS

1 heaped tsp butter
3 tbsp almond flour
1 tsp coconut flour
half a tsp baking powder

pinch of salt
1 white of a large egg
1 tbsp water

RECIPE

Place the butter in the base of your bowl or ramekin. Microwave for 20 seconds to melt the butter.

Add both types of flour, baking powder, pinch of salt, egg white and water.

Use a fork to stir and whisk the ingredients together until you have a smooth batter. Rest for a minute to thicken slightly.

Microwave for 1 min 30 secs. Run a knife around the edge and flip the roll onto a plate or board. Transfer to a rack to cool or slice in half and toast.

WAYS TO USE YOUR ROLLS

The pale bread roll can be cooled, sliced in half and used exactly like a normal roll. If you'd like your roll to be more browned on the top, you can always pop it in the oven (heated to 200C fan) for 5m.

If you're impatient, you can toast your roll before it has cooled. Simply cut in half, pop in the toaster and voila.

NUTRITIONAL INFORMATION PER SERVING

Calories 288 | Fat 16.8g | Net carbs 3.4g | Protein 24.8g

2-MIN TOASTED TEACAKE

Perfect served with lashings of butter on a cold afternoon!

. . . .

SERVES	TIME	CARBS	CALS
1	2M	3.4G	288

. . . .

INGREDIENTS

. . . .

1 heaped tsp butter
3 tbsp almond flour
1 tsp coconut flour
2 tsp erythritol

0.5 tsp baking powder
1/4 tsp ground cinnamon
1 white of a large egg
1 tbsp water

Place the butter in the base of your bowl or ramekin. Microwave for 20 seconds to melt the butter.

Add both types of flour, erythritol, baking powder, cinnamon, egg white and water.

Use a fork to stir and whisk the ingredients together until you have a smooth batter. Rest for a minute to thicken slightly.

Microwave for 1 min 30 secs. Run a knife around the edge and flip the roll onto a plate or board. Slice in half and pop in the toaster.

NUTRITIONAL INFORMATION PER SERVING

. . . .

Calories 288 | Fat 16.8g | Net carbs 3.4g | Protein 24.8g

A L O A F O F B R E A D

I've got two bread recipes for you here. The first, *Golden Flaxseed Bread* is made of almond flour and flaxseeds. It is most similar to a granary bread. The second, *Dark Seeded Bread* uses only seeds and is a rich dark bread in a rye style.

I make both in advance and keep them in the freezer to make toast. I use the *Golden Flaxseed Bread* as my day-to-day bread. It's great with butter and a huge variety of toppings. The *Dark Seeded Bread* I love with strong Scandinavian flavours – think Smoked Salmon and cream cheese or a strong cheese and my *Cauliflower Chutney*.

Speciality Ingredients

To make either bread, you'll need a few ingredients that you can't get in the supermarket.

For the *Golden Flaxseed Bread,* you'll need a finely ground almond flour. I recommend the one from Real Food Source.

Golden Flaxseeds are also needed. You can normally buy this from the supermarket, the brand I like is Yum and Yay. You can of course also buy it through my Amazon shop.

For both breads, psyllium husks are necessary. This is a fabulous ingredient that is important to hold the bread together. It is very fibrous and absorbs a lot of water, so is great for thickening shakes and sauces too.

For the *Dark Seeded Bread*, you also need ground flaxseeds. This is different from milled flaxseed. Ground flaxseed (also called flaxseed meal) is more like flour and is needed as the main ingredient in the *Dark Seeded Bread*.

Finally, the *Dark Seeded Bread* also needs inulin and vitamin C. Inulin is a natural fibre (from chicory root) that I use this in lots of other recipes too.

All these ingredients can be found easily on my Amazon Shop

www.helloketocookbook.com

GOLDEN FLAXSEED BREAD

Try this if you want to get a good consistency and crumb.

....

SERVES	TIME	CARBS	CALS
16	**1H 30M**	**1.2G**	**92**

....

INGREDIENTS

....

225g (7.9oz) almond flour
30g milled golden flaxseed
30g psyllium husk powder
1 tbsp baking powder
1 tsp salt
4 egg whites (large egg)
2 tbsp olive oil
200ml (7.1oz) warm water

Preheat the oven to 220C/200C fan. Line a large loaf tin with greaseproof paper and lightly oil.

In a large bowl, mix all the dry ingredients together thoroughly.

Break the eggs and separate the egg whites into a different bowl. Using a fork or hand whisk, whisk the egg whites for 2 minutes or until lightly foamy.

Add the oil and warm water to the dry ingredients and stir together. Fold in the egg whites. Use your hands to knead the dough for about 2 minutes. The mixture is very moist at first but gets dryer as you mix. After 2 minutes, it should come together easily to make a dough. If it's too sticky, add a little bit more psyllium husk.

Shape the dough into a loaf shape and place into the prepared loaf tin. Do not press in or flatten the loaf.

Bake for 1 hour in the oven. Reduce the heat to 180C/160C fan, Cover the bread with foil and keep baking for a further 20-30 mins. Lift the bread out of the pan & leave to cool.

When cooled, cut into 16 slices. The bread can be frozen in individual slices and reheated in the toaster.

NUTRITIONAL INFORMATION PER SERVING

....

Calories 92 | Fat 5.0g | Net carbs 1.2g | Protein 7.6g

DARK SEEDED BREAD

vegan / high protein / low carb

. . . .

SERVES	TIME	CARBS	CALS
16	**1H 30M**	**1.2G**	**86**

. . . .

INGREDIENTS

. . . .

150g (5.3oz) ground flaxseed

60g (2.1oz) sunflower seeds

30g (1.1oz) chia seeds

30g (1.1oz) psyllium husk powder

20g (0.7oz) inulin

6 tsp salt

4 tsp vitamin c

Pre-heat the oven to 210C/200C fan/400F/GAS 6. Line a baking tray with greaseproof paper or a silicone sheet.

Take a large bowl and mix all the dry ingredients together thoroughly.

Pour in 420ml water. Stir well for at least a minute. With wet hands, shape the dough into a sausage shape about 10"/25cm long. Cut a slit down the length of the dough. Bake in the oven for 90 minutes.

Transfer to a wire rack to cool. Cut into 20 thin slices and freeze until needed.

NOTES

. . . .

When cooled, cut into 16 slices. The bread can be frozen in individual slices and reheated in the toaster.

NUTRITIONAL INFORMATION PER SERVING

. . . .

Calories 86 | Fat 6.0g | Net carbs 1.2g | Protein 3.4g

TORTILLA FLATBREAD

A keto tortilla or flatbread is a fantastically versatile food item. You can serve them with a curry or stew, or make a delicious filling and turn it into a wrap. Even better, these flatbreads can be refrigerated or frozen, so you can always have one to hand.

Thanks to the psyllium husk, these wraps turn out extremely pliable, soft and chewy.

Your wraps they should keep fine in the fridge for a week. To reheat, microwave for 5 seconds per wrap or reheat in a frying pan. You can also freeze the wraps. Just defrost before using.

SOFT TORTILLA FLATBREAD

You need your heaviest frying pan to flatten these tortillas.

SERVES	TIME	CARBS	CALS
8	20M	1.5G	136

INGREDIENTS

150g (5.3oz) almond flour
6 tbsp psyllium husk powder
1 tsp baking powder
1 tsp salt
4 egg whites (large egg)
half a cup boiling water
1 tbsp olive oil

Mix the almond flour, psyllium, baking powder and salt together in a large bowl. Separate the eggs and mix the egg whites into the flour.

Add the boiling water a little at a time, stirring well. Once mixed, let the dough sit for 5 minutes (this is important for the psyllium to absorb the water).

Separate the dough into 8 balls. Place one of the balls between two large pieces of greaseproof paper. Using your heaviest frying pan, press down firmly on the dough ball. You can twist and press the frying pan a little bit to make it thinner. Your tortilla should be 2-3mm thick. Repeat with the other dough balls.

Lightly grease a frying pan with a little oil (you'll need to repeat this every 1-2 tortillas). When the pan is hot, add your first tortilla and cook for about 30 seconds each side. It should be lightly browned.

NUTRITIONAL INFORMATION PER SERVING

Calories 136 | Fat 5.1g | Net carbs 1.5g | Protein 10.5g

STAGE 2: ACTIVE KETO

Rule for Active Keto: Keep Daily Carbs below 40g.
(Yes that's the same as for the *Fire Up Challenge*, but it will be much easier as your body adjusts)

Huge congratulations for making it this far!

I know starting out on keto can be a rollercoaster ride as your body adjusts (and possibly resists) to the change of regime. All of that is now behind you and you'll be able to enjoy the freedom real keto gives you.

If you're still thinking that Active Keto is not freedom (because you still can't eat carbs!) then let me explain that the freedom comes from not wanting or needing carbs, and that is incredibly powerful. If you're not quite there yet, don't worry, sometimes reaching keto equilibrium takes a little bit more than a week. Carry on with *Active Keto* and the adjustment will come. You'll also start to feel truly motivated as the weight-loss starts and doesn't stop!

This is the workhorse of the keto plan. It's the phase where you'll lose weight and feel bursting with energy. You'll also naturally feel less hungry between meals and have less cravings for carbs.

If you've been good and steered clear of the sweet treats, your taste buds will have adjusted, and you'll love the chocolate and sweet treats that *Active Keto* allows.

UP TO 12 WEEKS OF ACTIVE KETO

The *Active Phase of Keto* can last for up to 12 weeks. Unlike many keto plans, I don't think it's forever. I believe that good healthy starchy carbs do have a place in a healthy balanced diet and that's why after 12 weeks of *Active Keto,* you then move to *The Healthy Sugar-Free Lifestyle.* As the name suggests, the sugar-free lifestyle is a change for life. You'll find it easy to move to this after doing keto. The key take-away is that you'll still lose or maintain weight on the sugar-free lifestyle, and you will be free of the sugar rollercoaster for good.

If you find that the weight-loss aspects are no longer needed, then feel free to move on to the next stage.

It's easier to do your 12 weeks of *Active Keto* all in one go, but if you have a holiday, a wedding or a blip, then you can stop and start. After a pause, there's a few tricky days of getting back on track and then it's easy again. In the *Sugar-free lifestyle* section of the book, there is a guide to recovering from a blip that can also be used for *Active Keto.*

What to expect?

There are two major benefits to being in *Active Keto*:

Weight-loss

The first and probably the one that you feel is most important is Weight loss. Unlike with other forms of diet, the weight-loss you achieve is predictable and sustained when you are on Active Keto.

Depending on how far you are from your target weight, the weight-loss you will achieve is between one and three pounds a week. As a rough guide, you can expect your weight-loss to be about a pound a week if you've got less than seven pounds of weight to lose to reach a healthy BMI. If you've got between seven pounds and a stone to lose then you'll lose about 2 pounds a week. Anything more than a stone to lose and you should lose upwards of three pounds a week.

Why is it so predictable? Your body cannot store any excess fat that you consume. Your body uses the fat that you eat AND your body fat for energy, hence why you always lose the same amount of body fat each week.

Energy & Mood

Possibly even more important than weight-loss is how good you feel. You might not even notice until you have a blip and you accidentally eat a pizza or go out for a curry. And then you'll feel Bloated, Apathetic and Blue. I call it feeling BAB, and you soon realise that this is not something you want to experience so you learn to avoid.

The change in energy and mood is caused by the fact that your blood sugar levels are stable at a low but safe level. No more sugar rush and the blues that follow. Your natural state is this level of energy and mood and you have now reached it. Enjoy and remember that feeling if you ever fancy stopping. It's a great motivator to keep going.

What to do if things go wrong?

Everyone has a blip now and again. It could be your social life interfering with your keto plan, or it could be an illness. Any illness totally knocks you off track with any diet. I know it's frustrating but listen to your body. You may well start to crave carbs if you have a virus or a cold. The best thing to do is not beat yourself up about this. Rest and wait until you are fully recovered and then get back on track. It takes a few days to get back into the keto zone but it's much easier than when you're first starting out.

Taking MCT oil during Active Keto

If you've already been taking MCT oil during *Fire Up*, then you'll be starting to realise how much it supports you in resisting cravings and curbing your appetite. Ideally, you should take 2-3 tsp about an hour before breakfast and the same before lunch.

THE SIMILARITIES BETWEEN KETO & 5:2 / FASTING

When I first started doing keto, I didn't understand how keto and fasting could be related. They are so different. When I've done 5:2 before, I've felt like my insides are "clawing their way out" with hunger. It's not a pleasant feeling and one of the reasons that although I still support

5:2ers (it's a fantastic weight-loss regime but it's hard) I don't do it myself.

The key to understanding the way they both work on the body is to understand the effect that both diets have on your blood sugar levels.

Fasting triggers a hormonal and fat-loss reaction in the body. Your body will use the simplest energy stores first. This is ALWAYS carbohydrates. Both when you fast AND when you stop eating carbs, you enter a semi-fasting state and your blood glucose levels fall. This triggers the release of metabolic fuels from the body's store of fat. The metabolic effect of fasting and of carbohydrate restriction are fundamentally the same.

Additionally, when you have been following *Active Keto* for a few weeks, you'll notice that you'll naturally be able to go for longer without food. This is again because your blood sugar levels are stable and low. You will only feel the need to eat when your released fat stores are depleted.

If you find that you are forcing yourself to eat because it's breakfast time or lunchtime, then you are ready to move to a more advanced stage which combines keto and fasting.

Don't worry if this is something that you don't feel comfortable with, or simply doesn't fit in with your life, you are perfectly fine to just continue with Active Keto. But if you're thinking about progressing, then Window Eating Keto is a great way to up your game.

STEPPING UP THE PACE WITH WINDOW EATING

It's amazing what your body can do when you step off the sugar and carb rollercoaster. Your blood sugar is a maintained at a low but safe level. One huge advantage of this is that you can go longer without food easily and you won't feel deprived. If you don't believe me, try skipping breakfast one day and see how easily you can get through to lunch.

Window Eating is when you only eat during certain hours of the day. A common Window Eating regime is to only eat between 12pm and 8pm. But it is also extremely effective to do it between 10am and 8pm.

First and foremost, don't feel that you have to Window Eat every day. Just a few days a week or Monday to Friday are absolutely fine.

There are two equally important parts to window eating. The first is the simple restriction to not eat after 8pm. This gives you plenty of time to eat your evening meal and feel fully satiated, but it's a nice simple rule that stops you snacking unnecessarily in the evening.

And the other part is to wait until either 10am or 12pm until you eat your first meal of the day. This means that you'll naturally be cutting down to 2 meals a day. Either brunch and dinner or lunch and dinner. In the morning you'll find your natural hunger will kick in later and later as it is not ruled by your blood sugar.

If you're taking MCT Oil, then this also helps enormously, and you can have this before the eating window opens. The MCT oil stops any nagging hunger and also makes you less hungry during the afternoon. MCT oil should be taken about an hour before you eat – at 9am or 11am. Note: if you are window eating you will only have MCT oil once a day. Each serving will be 3 tsp / 1 tbsp.

If you're reading this and thinking I'll never be able to manage that, then know that when I was 5:2-ing with a 14 hour fast I was absolutely starving by 10am. Now I manage fasting until 12pm (with MCT oil at 11am) with ease. I am not ravenous at lunch but really enjoy it and I will snack if I want to in the afternoon, but find I rarely need it.

It's interesting to note that Window Eating without carb restriction is a diet regime in its own right. But it's much harder to maintain when eating carbs as you are on the blood sugar roller-coaster again.

MEAL PLANS FOR ACTIVE KETO

There's 3 weeks of Meal Plans for *Active Keto* and a *Vegetarian Active Keto* Plan. Each is followed by a Shopping List.

Each Meal Plan comes in at under 30g Carbs per day. You can add low carb snacks up to a max of 40g Carbs per day.

You can follow the Meal Plans exactly or feel free to 'Mix & Match' with other recipes that take your fancy.

ACTIVE KETO [WEEK 1] MEAL PLAN

Monday	Tuesday	Weds	Thursday	Friday	Saturday	Sunday
Magnificent Muesli 2.6g carbs (page 114)	Magnificent Muesli 2.6g carbs (page 114)	Magnificent Muesli 2.6g carbs (page 114)	Magnificent Muesli 2.6g carbs (page 114)	Magnificent Muesli 2.6g carbs (page 114)	Smoked Salmon & Eggs 2.5g carbs (page 119)	Super Fruit Smoothie 3.8g carbs (page 110)
Prawn Salad Topped with Seeds 15.5g carbs (page 125)	Slow Onion Soup 12.8g carbs (page 141)	Slow Onion Soup 12.8g carbs (page 141)	Avocado, Egg & Cashew Nut Lunchbox 12.5g carbs (page 127)	Avocado, Egg & Cashew Nut Lunchbox 12.5g carbs (page 127)	Houmous Stuffed Pepper 11g carbs (page 133)	Creamy Salmon & Leek Bowl 14.9g carbs (page 160)
Chinese Steak Salad 9.8g carbs (page 149)	Mexican Pulled Pork 9.5g carbs (page 172)	Chilli Steak Ramen 10.5g carbs (page 159)	Chilli Steak Ramen 10.5g carbs (page 159)	Mexican Pulled Pork 9.5g carbs (page 172)	Cambodian Chicken 15.8g carbs (page 161)	Best Beef Chilli 11.3g carbs (page 170)
28g carbs	25.1g carbs	26g carbs	25.7g carbs	24.7g carbs	29.3g carbs	30.2g carbs

ACTIVE KETO [WEEK 1]

FRUIT & VEGETABLES
white onion(s) / frozen onions
red onions
shallots
red pepper / mixed peppers
green pepper / mixed peppers
cauliflower
carrots
red chillies
beansprouts
leeks
tomatoes
cherry tomatoes
cucumber
salad leaves
spring (green) onions
avocados
baby spinach leaves
fresh coriander leaves
radishes
lemons
lime(s)
pomegranate seeds

DAIRY & EGGS
large eggs
butter
almond milk
creme fraiche
houmous

MEAT, CHICKEN & FISH
smoked salmon
salmon fillets
chicken thighs
sirloin steak
minced (ground) beef 5% fat
pork shoulder joint
beef stock

HERBS & SPICES
paprika / smoked paprika
turmeric
chilli powder
cumin
ground coriander
chilli (red pepper) flakes
bay leaves
ground cinnamon
oregano (dried)
dried onion
chipotle flakes
dried thyme

NUTS & SEEDS
sunflower seeds
pumpkin seeds
chia seeds
sesame seeds
desiccated coconut
flaked coconut
cashews
whole almonds
macadamia nuts

OIL & VINEGAR
olive oil
white wine vinegar
rice vinegar

STORE CUPBOARD
garlic paste
ginger paste
tomato paste
tomato ketchup
coconut milk
1 can chopped tomatoes
vegetable stock
red wine
1 can kidney beans
baking powder
cocoa powder
vanilla extract

WORLD FOODS
lemongrass paste
sriracha hot sauce
galangal paste
tamarind paste
fish sauce
konjac noodles
light soy sauce
kimchee

FROZEN
frozen mixed berries
frozen prawns (shrimp)

SPECIALITY
inulin
psyllium husk powder
almond flour
erythritol
milled golden flaxseed
erythritol

ACTIVE KETO [WEEK 2] MEAL PLAN

	Monday	Tuesday	Weds	Thursday	Friday	Saturday	Sunday
	Nuts & Seeds Granola 3.3g carbs (page 113)	Nuts & Seeds Granola 3.3g carbs (page 113)	Nuts & Seeds Granola 3.3g carbs (page 113)	Nuts & Seeds Granola 3.3g carbs (page 113)	Nuts & Seeds Granola 3.3g carbs (page 113)	2m Toasted Teacake with sugar-free jam 4.8g carbs (pg 52,189)	Big Veggie Breakfast 4.7g carbs (page 117)
	Creamy Tomato Soup 7.6g carbs (page 138)	Creamy Tomato Soup 7.6g carbs (page 138)	Avocado, Egg & Cashew Nut Lunchbox 12.5g carbs (page 127)	Protein Packed Tuna Salad 5.1g carbs (page 124)	Protein Packed Tuna Salad 5.1g carbs (page 124)	Creamy Mushrooms on Toast 5.9g carbs (page 131)	Creamy Mushrooms on Toast 5.9g carbs (page 131)
	Fresh Chicken Curry 14.9g carbs (page 169)	Fresh Chicken Curry 14.9g carbs (page 169)	Steak and Feta Salad 7.9g carbs (page 146)	Steak and Feta Salad 7.9g carbs (page 146)	Prawn Thai Fragrant Curry 17.4g carbs (page 157)	Chilli Steak Ramen 10.5g carbs (page 159)	Katsu Chicken Curry 7.5g carbs (page 153)
	25.8g carbs	25.8g carbs	23.7g carbs	16.4g carbs	25.9g carbs	21.3g carbs	18.1g carbs

ACTIVE KETO [WEEK 2]

FRUIT & VEGETABLES
white onion(s) / frozen onions
red onions
red pepper / frozen peppers
chestnut mushrooms
flat mushrooms
broccoli florets
red chillies
green chillies
beansprouts
tomatoes
cherry tomatoes
salad leaves
baby spinach leaves
spring (green) onions
2 avocados
fresh coriander leaves
2 limes
2 lemons

DAIRY & EGGS
large eggs
cream cheese
butter
feta
double cream

MEAT, CHICKEN & FISH
3 chicken breast fillets
chicken stock
sirloin steak
beef stock

HERBS & SPICES
paprika
turmeric
chilli powder
cumin
ground coriander
mild curry powder
dried mixed herbs
smoked paprika
ground cinnamon
oregano (dried)
dried onion
chipotle flakes

NUTS & SEEDS
sunflower seeds

pumpkin seeds
ground almonds
chia seeds
cashews
macadamia nuts
pecans
chopped mixed nuts

OIL & VINEGAR
olive oil / mild olive oil
balsamic vinegar
white wine vinegar
rice vinegar

STORE CUPBOARD
garlic paste
ginger paste
tomato paste
tomato ketchup
1 can coconut milk
2 cans chopped tomatoes
1 can tuna
palm sugar
Worcestershire sauce
vegetarian stock powder
white wine
baking powder
vanilla paste

WORLD FOODS
lemongrass paste
sriracha hot sauce
fish sauce
konjac noodles
soy sauce / light soy sayce
kimchee

FROZEN
frozen mixed berries
frozen king prawns (shrimp)

SPECIALITY
coconut flour
psyllium husk powder
erythritol
almond flour
erythritol
milled golden flaxseed
erythritol

ACTIVE KETO [WEEK 3] MEAL PLAN

Day	Breakfast	Lunch	Dinner	Total
Monday	Super Fruit Smoothie 3.8g carbs (page 110)	Greek Lunchbox Salad with Pine Nuts 12.1g carbs (page 126)	Chicken Korma 10.3g carbs (page 171)	26.3g carbs
Tuesday	Chocolate Shake 1.8g carbs (page 109)	Easy Bake Goats Cheese Frittata 5.7g carbs (page 123)	Chicken Korma 10.3g carbs (page 171)	18g carbs
Weds	Super Veg Smoothie 1.5g carbs (page 111)	Easy Bake Goats Cheese Frittata 5.7g carbs (page 123)	Pork & Shiitake Mushroom Stir Fry 13.6g carbs (page 147)	21g carbs
Thursday	Chocolate Shake 1.8g carbs (page 109)	Protein Packed Tuna Salad 5.1g carbs (page 124)	Pork & Shiitake Mushroom Stir Fry 13.6g carbs (page 147)	20.7g carbs
Friday	Almond & Flaxseed Porridge 2.2g carbs (page 112)	Protein Packed Tuna Salad 5.1g carbs (page 124)	Creamy Salmon & Leek Bowl 14.9g carbs (page 160)	22.3g carbs
Saturday	Smoked Salmon & Eggs 2.5g carbs (page 119)	Chinese Steak Salad 9.8g carbs (page 149)	Cod Ramen with Naked Noodles 12g carbs (page 163)	24.3g carbs
Sunday	2 Minute Bread Roll 3.3g carbs (page 51)	Chinese Steak Salad 9.8g carbs (page 149)	Healthy Fried Chicken 11.6g carbs (page 167)	24.8g carbs

ACTIVE KETO [WEEK 3]

FRUIT & VEGETABLES
white onion(s) / frozen onions
red onions
shallots
green pepper / frozen peppers
carrot
broccoli florets
beansprouts
leeks
pak choi
shiitake mushrooms

cherry tomatoes
salad leaves
baby spinach leaves
spring (green) onions
1 avocado
radishes
2 lemons

DAIRY & EGGS
large eggs
cream cheese
goats cheese
butter
buttermilk
creme fraiche
natural greek yogurt
feta
almond milk

MEAT, CHICKEN & FISH
chicken breast fillets
smoked salmon
salmon fillets
cod fillets
2 sirloin steaks
2 pork loin steaks

HERBS & SPICES
paprika
turmeric
chilli powder
cumin
ground coriander
dried fenugreek leaves
cayenne pepper
dried onion

NUTS & SEEDS
pinenuts
sesame seeds
chia seeds

OIL & VINEGAR
olive oil
coconut oil
toasted sesame oil
rapeseed oil
balsamic vinegar
white wine vinegar
rice vinegar

STORE CUPBOARD
garlic paste
ginger paste
tomato paste
tomato ketchup
Worcestershire sauce
vegetable stock
1 can coconut milk
1 can tuna
cocoa powder
English mustard
sun-dried tomatoes in oil
baking powder

WORLD FOODS
mirin
fish sauce
konjac noodles
oyster sauce
soy sauce / light soy sauce
gram flour

FROZEN
frozen mixed berries

SPECIALITY
coconut flour
psyllium husk powder
almond flour
erythritol
milled golden flaxseed
your favourite protein powder

ACTIVE KETO VEGETARIAN MEAL PLAN

	Monday	Tuesday	Weds	Thursday	Friday	Saturday	Sunday
	Nuts & Seeds Granola 3.3g carbs (page 113)	Magnificent Muesli 2.6g carbs (page 114)	Nuts & Seeds Granola 3.3g carbs (page 113)	Magnificent Muesli 2.6g carbs (page 114)	Nuts & Seeds Granola 3.3g carbs (page 113)	Perfect Pancakes 3 Ways 0.8g carbs (page 118)	Perfect Pancakes 3 Ways 0.8g carbs (page 118)
	Greek Lunch-box Salad with Pine Nuts 12.1g carbs (page 126)	Easy Bake Goats Cheese Frittata 5.7g carbs (page 123)	Easy Bake Goats Cheese Frittata 5.7g carbs (page 123)	Avocado, Egg & Cashew Nut Lunchbox 12.5g carbs (page 127)	Greek Lunch-box Salad with Pine Nuts 12.1g carbs (page 126)	Lazy Carrot and Coriander 12.9g carbs (page 137)	Lazy Carrot and Coriander 12.9g carbs (page 137)
	Aubergine, Spinach & Paneer Curry 13.6g carbs (page 173)	Cauliflower Tofu Curry 10.8g carbs (page 148)	Cauliflower Tofu Curry 10.8g carbs (page 148)	Aubergine, Spinach & Paneer Curry 13.6g carbs (page 173)	Smashed Avocado & Poached Egg 8.1g carbs (page 132)	Creamy Mushrooms on Toast 5.9g carbs (page 131)	Creamy Mushrooms on Toast 5.9g carbs (page 131)
	29g carbs	19.3g carbs	19.9g carbs	28.7g carbs	23.6g carbs	19.7g carbs	19.7g carbs

ACTIVE KETO [VEGGIE]

FRUIT & VEGETABLES
white onion(s) / frozen onions
red onions
cauliflower
chestnut mushrooms
carrots
large aubergine

tomatoes
cherry tomatoes
salad leaves
baby spinach leaves
spring (green) onions
1 avocados

2 lemons

DAIRY & EGGS
paneer cheese
large eggs
cream cheese
goats cheese
natural greek yogurt
butter
feta
almond milk
tofu

HERBS & SPICES
turmeric
cumin
ground coriander
dried mixed herbs
ground cinnamon
garam massala
dried onion
chilli flakes
curry leaves
cumin seeds
mustard seeds
nigella seeds

NUTS & SEEDS
pinenuts
sunflower seeds
pumpkin seeds
ground almonds
chia seeds

flaked coconut
cashews
whole almonds
macadamia nuts
pecans
chopped mixed nuts

OIL & VINEGAR
olive oil
mild olive oil
balsamic vinegar
white wine vinegar
rice vinegar

STORE CUPBOARD
garlic paste
ginger paste
tomato paste
tomato ketchup
vegetable stock
coconut milk
English mustard
sun-dried tomatoes in oil
white wine
baking powder
vanilla extract
vanilla paste

WORLD FOODS
light soy sauce
soy sauce

SPECIALITY
inulin
psyllium husk powder
erythritol
almond flour
erythritol
milled golden flaxseed
erythritol

HELP! I'VE GOT A SWEET TOOTH

Me too! I do totally understand this as I always fancy something sweet after meals. Some people find that they just don't need sweet stuff in their lives – but I'm not one of them.

Luckily for us, the craving for sweetness has nothing to do with needing a sugar-hit, it's not a need it's a want. And that craving can be satiated with sugar-free treats and chocolate made from sweeteners.

We really are living in a miraculous age for sweeteners. And finally, I have found what I consider to be the holy grail for sweetness with no funny taste or side effects. I've found that making my own sugar-free and low carb chocolate is the answer. You may also find that my sugar-free mug cake or puddings will help with your cravings.

There's a couple of things going on here. If you've successfully made it through the Fire Up phase as a 'sugar addict' you'll have found it harder than most. Not only are you battling with your sweet tooth but also with the addictive qualities of the sugar itself. That is why it is important to have a week with absolutely no sweetness in it, to rid yourself of the ups and downs of your need for sugar. The good news is that after you have beaten off the addictive properties of sugar, and are happily maintaining your sugar levels at a stable low level, then you can add 'sweet' things back into your diet, as long as they are sweetened without sugars.

This is where my delicious chocolates come in. I eat two or three EVERY SINGLE DAY. There's a few tricks and some non-supermarket ingredients (but I will give you the Amazon links on www.helloketocookbook.com)

Have you seen the ridiculously expensive sugar-free chocolate bars you can buy now? Make your own - you will not look back… Seriously this has been the most important thing for me to NOT FEEL DEPRIVED and becoming a successful Keto-er.

Before we start with making the chocolates themselves, let's look a little bit more at sweeteners and also at the sweetener I recommend for making chocolate.

Understanding sweeteners

There's a huge amount of conflicting advice on sweeteners – how they work, whether they are natural, whether they are good for you and how they taste.

I'm going to cut through all the rubbish and make a couple of recommendations.

There are two basic types of sweeteners: artificial and "natural". Artificial are made from chemical ingredients, natural are derived from food sources. I put natural in quotes because natural in this case is not necessarily better.

There are probably many "artificial" things that you take during your daily life – vitamins, pain killers and all medication are "artificial" so don't just dismiss them out of hand. Likewise, "natural" sweeteners go through chemical manipulation to turn it into the sweetener. And don't forget, sugar is also chemically treated to turn it from the beet or cane into its crystalline form and we don't consider sugar to be unnatural.

The 3 most important factors in choosing a sweetener

1   Good Taste (no aftertaste and as similar as possible to sugar)

2   Lack of side effects

3   Does not raise your blood sugar

I'm going to suggest two sweeteners that I think you need in your life. Why more than one? Because some sweeteners work better with different foods or are better for baking.

Erythritol
Erythritol is in the polyol sweetener family. There's a few of them about – xylitol, maltiol, sorbitol... But erythritol is by far the best and the only one you need. First and foremost, it has the best taste. No aftertaste, no cooling effect. It's great in cooking. Erythritol and xylitol are both now available in your supermarket. But don't be fooled by the xylitol – it causes digestive upset AND is poisonous to cats and dogs! You should be able to buy granulated erythritol in the supermarket, and this is great for most things. However, if you plan on making my chocolate recipes then you need powdered erythritol (granulated erythritol

tastes gritty in chocolate) and so far, I haven't found this in the supermarket.

The one I love (and use for everything!) is by NKD living and the link can be found on my Amazon shop

https://www.helloketocookbook.com

Erythritol is about a third less sweet than sugar BUT your taste buds are changing, and you won't like things as sweet anymore. In my recipes, we use the same amount of erythritol as you would use sugar. Easy!

Stevia

Everyone has heard of stevia. But if you are one of those people that goes – 'Yuck it's horrible. Never eating that!' then read on as we'll be using it in very specific circumstances to make sure you never get that taste.

If you read the packet of stevia-based sweeteners in a granulated or powder form, you'll be surprised to note that the stevia only makes up a tiny proportion, the rest is erythritol. Stevia is a very concentrated sweetener and the erythritol balances it out, so it is about the same sweetness as sugar.

The key to using stevia is that it can be combined with some foods to give a natural sweetness but has a really strong unpleasant taste if mixed with others.

Stevia based sweeteners can be used to sweeten dairy (yogurt) and fruit (jam) but not chocolate and baked goods. Just follow this rule and you'll be fine. Of course, erythritol can sweeten all these things with no aftertaste so you can skip the stevia altogether if you prefer.

THE ART OF MAKING CHOCOLATE

There are definitely a few techniques to making chocolate that you might not be used to. None of these are hard at all. It's just understanding that a 'bung-it-all-in' approach will not work with chocolate.

The first thing to understand is that you cannot allow any water to mix with the chocolate. That means no milk, no dissolving the erythritol in water and simply no ingredients that contain more than a smidge of water. Adding water to melted chocolate, immediately causes the chocolate to seize and the chocolate does not then set correctly, it's more fudgey.

Don't be scared of the double boiler. It's just a small pan of boiling water with a larger bowl (like a pyrex) sitting on the top. The water does not touch the bottom of the bowl, it is the steam from the boiling water that melts the chocolate.

Finally, the erythritol does not dissolve easily in the chocolate. If not approached with a little care, the erythritol can crystallize and you don't get the smooth consistency. To help with this, we mix the erythritol with the inulin before adding to the melted chocolate a little at a time. We also add a pinch of sunflower lecithin, a natural emulsifier which helps the erythritol mix into the chocolate.

Good chocolate is all about a smooth creamy texture which is why you should approach your first batch with a little bit of care and the right ingredients to hand. Once you've learnt the technique however, it's quick and easy.

Special Ingredients

There are several special ingredients that you need to buy and they are all available here:

www.helloketocookbook.com

The two crucial parts are cocoa butter and cocoa mass. The two essentials for chocolate. They smell like chocolate but don't taste like it as they are unsweetened. Blending them with the right sweetener and flavourings are how you add the magic to make perfect keto-friendly chocolates.

CHOCOLATE RECIPES

Dark Chocolate Hazelnuts

Milk Chocolate Stars

Caramel Hearts

Praline Shells

Chocolate Peanut Butter Swirls

Chocolate Orange

DARK CHOCOLATE HAZELNUTS

Use a 15-hole chocolate tray for this recipe.

SERVES	TIME	CARBS	CALS
8	10M	0.7G	86

INGREDIENTS

40g (1.4oz) cocoa butter
30g (1.1oz) cocoa mass
20g (0.7oz) erythritol
10g (0.4oz) inulin

15 whole hazelnuts
pinch of salt
pinch of sunflower lecithin

Place the cocoa butter and half the cocoa mass in a glass bowl. We're going to put it over a saucepan of boiling water in a minute so make sure it's big enough.

In a separate (small) bowl, mix the erythritol and inulin. Place the chocolate bowl over a small saucepan of simmering water and keep stirring until all melted and combined.

Add the erythritol and inulin mix a little bit at a time. Use a balloon whisk to thoroughly mix each time. This is crucial as the erythritol could easily crystallize during this phase.

Remove from the heat. Stir in a pinch of salt and a pinch of sunflower lecithin (this helps the ingredients to combine and be smooth). Finally stir in the rest of the cocoa mass.

When the cocoa mass is fully integrated, pour a little (each mould should be about one third full) of the chocolate into each mould.

Gently push a hazelnut into each chocolate. Pour over the rest of the chocolate mixture. Refrigerate to set.

This recipe makes 100g of chocolate or 15 chocolates. One serving is two chocolates.

NUTRITIONAL INFORMATION PER SERVING

Calories 86 | Fat 8.6g | Net carbs 0.7g | Protein 0.9g

MILK CHOCOLATE STARS

I use a silicone "star" tray to make these chocolates.

SERVES	TIME	CARBS	CALS
8	5M	1.2G	63

INGREDIENTS

35g (1.2oz) cocoa butter
20g (0.7oz) cocoa mass
20g (0.7oz) erythritol
10g (0.4oz) inulin

15g (0.5oz) whole milk powder
pinch of salt
pinch of sunflower lecithin

Place the cocoa butter and half the cocoa mass in a glass bowl. We're going to put it over a saucepan of boiling water in a minute so make sure it's big enough.

In a separate (small) bowl, mix the erythritol and inulin together.

Place the chocolate bowl over a small saucepan of simmering water and keep stirring until all melted and combined.

Add the erythritol and inulin mix a little bit at a time. Use a balloon whisk to thoroughly mix each time. This is crucial as the erythritol could easily crystallize during this phase.

Next add the milk powder a little at a time, whisking again. Remove from the heat. Stir in a pinch of salt and a pinch of sunflower lecithin (this helps the ingredients to combine and be smooth). Finally stir in the rest of the cocoa mass.

When the cocoa mass is fully integrated, pour the chocolate mixture into the moulds. Refrigerate to set.

This recipe makes 100g of chocolate or 15 stars. One serving is two chocolates.

NUTRITIONAL INFORMATION PER SERVING

Calories 63 | Fat 6.2g | Net carbs 1.2g | Protein 1.0g

CARAMEL HEARTS

vegetarian / low carb

. . . .

SERVES	TIME	CARBS	CALS
8	**10M**	**0.9G**	**75**

. . . .

INGREDIENTS

. . . .

30g (1.1oz) cocoa butter
20g (0.7oz) cocoa mass
10g (0.4oz) milk powder
10g (0.4oz) erythritol
5g (0.2oz) inulin

pinch of sunflower lecithin
20g (0.7oz) butter
1 tsp Monin Caramel Sugar
Free Syrup
10g (0.4oz) inulin

Place the cocoa butter and cocoa mass in a glass bowl. We're going to put it over a saucepan of boiling water in a minute so make sure it's big enough.

In a separate (small) bowl, mix the erythritol, inulin and sunflower lecithin together.

Place the chocolate bowl over a small saucepan of simmering water and keep stirring until melted / combined.

Add the erythritol and inulin mix a little bit at a time. When the mix is fully combined, half fill each of your chocolate moulds with the mixture, reserving at least a quarter for finishing off the chocolates.

Swirl the mixture round the mould so it goes up the sides. Refrigerate and swirl every 2 minutes until set.

Meanwhile, heat the butter in the microwave until melted. Stir in the inulin and caramel. Distribute the caramel sauce between the moulds and refrigerate for a few minutes.

Finally, pour the remaining chocolate over the caramel to seal the chocolate, tipping each from side to side to distribute the chocolate evenly.

NUTRITIONAL INFORMATION PER SERVING

. . . .

Calories 75 | Fat 7.5g | Net carbs 0.9g | Protein 0.8g

PRALINE SHELLS

vegetarian / low carb

....

SERVES	TIME	CARBS	CALS
8	5 M	1.4 G	58

....

INGREDIENTS

....

30g (1.1oz) cocoa butter
20g (0.7oz) cocoa mass
a few drops almond extract
20g (0.7oz) milk powder

15g (0.5oz) erythritol
5g (0.2oz) inulin
pinch of sunflower lecithin
20g almonds, ground or finely chopped

Place the cocoa butter, cocoa mass and almond extract in a glass bowl. We're going to put it over a saucepan of boiling water in a minute so make sure it's big enough.

In a separate (small) bowl, mix the milk powder, erythritol, inulin and sunflower lecithin together.

Place the chocolate bowl over a small saucepan of simmering water and keep stirring until all melted and combined.

Add the powdered mix a little bit at a time.

Finally stir in the finely chopped almonds.

Fill your chocolate shell moulds with the chocolate.

Refrigerate to set.

NUTRITIONAL INFORMATION PER SERVING

....

Calories 58 | Fat 5.7g | Net carbs 1.4g | Protein 1.2g

CHOCOLATE PEANUT BUTTER SWIRLS

SERVES	TIME	CARBS	CALS
8	**5 M**	**1.4 G**	**7 7**

INGREDIENTS

30g (1.1oz) cocoa butter
20g (0.7oz) cocoa mass
30g (1.1oz) peanut butter
(no added sugar)
half a tsp vanilla paste

10g (0.4oz) erythritol
5g (0.2oz) inulin
pinch of sunflower lecithin
10g (0.4oz) whole milk
powder

Place the cocoa butter, cocoa mass, peanut butter and vanilla paste in a glass bowl. We're going to put it over a saucepan of boiling water in a minute so make sure it's big enough.

In a separate (small) bowl, mix the erythritol, inulin and sunflower lecithin together.

Place the chocolate bowl over a small saucepan of simmering water and keep stirring until all melted and combined.

Add the erythritol and inulin mix a little bit at a time. When the mix is fully combined, half fill each of your chocolate moulds with the mixture.

Place the chocolate bowl back over the saucepan and add the milk powder, stirring well to combine.

Fill up your chocolate moulds with the rest of the chocolate.

Use a cocktail stick or similar to swirl the chocolate together - just one little swirl per chocolate is enough.

Refrigerate to set. One serving is 2 chocolates.

NUTRITIONAL INFORMATION PER SERVING

Calories 77 | Fat 7.4g | Net carbs 1.4g | Protein 1.8g

CHOCOLATE ORANGE

vegan / low carb

SERVES	TIME	CARBS	CALS
8	**5M**	**0.5G**	**69**

INGREDIENTS

40g (1.4oz) cocoa butter   pinch of salt
30g (1.1oz) cocoa mass   10g (0.4oz) inulin
half a tsp orange essence   pinch of sunflower lecithin
20g (0.7oz) erythritol

Place the cocoa butter, cocoa mass and orange essence in a glass bowl. We're going to put it over a saucepan of boiling water in a minute so make sure it's big enough.

In a separate (small) bowl, mix the erythritol, inulin, salt and sunflower lecithin together.

Place the chocolate bowl over a small saucepan of simmering water and keep stirring until all melted and combined.

Add the erythritol and inulin mix a little bit at a time. When the mix is fully combined, fill each of your chocolate moulds with the mixture.

Refrigerate to set.

NOTES

The recipe makes 100g of chocolate and is enough to fill a 15-hole mould.

One serving is 2 chocolates.

NUTRITIONAL INFORMATION PER SERVING

Calories 69 | Fat 7.0g | Net carbs 0.5g | Protein 0.5g

STAGE 3: SUGAR FREE LIFESTYLE

The *Sugar Free Lifestyle* is a natural plateau of perfect healthy living. It's a great place to be. You're full of boundless energy. And able to enjoy some of your favourite starchy carbs again.

Why no sugar?

Quite simply, sugar is addictive. It changes your brain chemistry to compel you to eat more despite the harmful consequences. If you start to add sugar regularly to your diet, that horrible sugar rollercoaster gets started again and you can't get off it again without going "cold turkey".

If you do find yourself slowly upping your sugar intake so that you are having it every day then you need to go back to Active Keto for several days to shake it off again. Read the section on recovering from a blowout and follow that advice to get you back on track.

Incorporating Starchy Carbs

One 'Good Carb' Meal Per Day, preferably Dinner

On most days, you should limit your starchy carbs to one meal a day, preferably your evening meal. This doesn't mean that you can't occasionally have two starchy meals in a day or swap lunch for dinner. Just that on a normal day, you should have a carb-free breakfast (or skip breakfast), a salad or soup for lunch (with plenty of protein and healthy fats) and a balanced evening meal with good carbs, plenty of protein and healthy fats.

GOOD CARBS VS BAD CARBS

The simple rule is to avoid white carbs – white bread, sugar etc – but to allow brown and coloured carbs back into your day.

'White' Carbs to avoid:

Flour, rice, potatoes, pasta, breakfast cereals and other processed grains

White or highly processed brown bread

Replace with:

Basmati rice, new potatoes

lentils and beans

Rye or pumpernickel bread

THE GOOD CARB LIST

1 Basmati Rice

Basmati rice is a great carbohydrate. Both brown and white basmati are available, with brown basmati containing slightly more fibre. If you find the cooking time for brown basmati is off-putting, try buying pouches of pre-steamed rice that go from packet to plate in 2 minutes flat. I like Tilda Brown Basmati rice as it has no unexpected ingredients.

2 Oats

Oats contain a very special and unique ingredient: beta-glucan. Beta-glucan is a type of fibre that means our bodies digest the carbohydrate more slowly and evenly. Oats therefore release their energy more slowly than other carbs and keep us fuller for longer. Oats are particularly good as a breakfast ingredient as they are so filling. Porridge oats are the standard oats we buy for porridge. Be careful to avoid 'quick' or 'express' oats as these have been overly processed with a lot of the goodness removed. Jumbo oats are bigger than porridge oats and have an even lower sugar load. They are also known as whole, traditional or old-fashioned oats. Oat bran is the most concentrated form of beta-glucan. It's finely milled and is a great baking ingredient.

3 Potatoes

Choosing the right sort of potatoes is crucial. New potatoes boiled in their skins and a potato baked in its skin are good carbs. Mashed potato and chips are bad carbs. They key is in the skin, which adds fibre, texture and flavour. A good portion size is 150g (5oz) – 3–4 new potatoes or a small jacket potato.

This means that the all-time winter warmer of jacket potato, baked beans and cheese is a good option... just don't forget to eat the potato skin.

4 Butternut Squash

Butternut squash has a much lower impact on blood sugar than similar foods such as sweet potato and pumpkin. It's tasty and naturally sweet and goes really well in a range of vegetarian dishes or as a side dish with meat or fish.

5 Lentils

Lentils are an amazing blend of good carbohydrate and protein. They are also extremely versatile. Puy lentils are great in all kinds of stews and salads, adding a unique nutty flavour and texture. Red and brown lentils are used in a lot of Indian cooking. They make a great main vegetarian dish.

6 Quinoa

Quinoa is another food that mixes carbohydrate and protein. A simple grain without much taste of its own, use it as a meal accompaniment or anywhere you might previously have used couscous.

7 Chickpeas

Chickpeas are one of the most versatile and well balanced of the foods that mix carbs, fibre and protein. Use them to make falafel or in stews.

8 Beans

Kidney beans, cannellini beans – even baked beans – they're all good. If you're buying baked beans, check the ingredients list for too many nasties – look for varieties with reduced sugar and salt.

CONTINUE TO FOLLOW WINDOW EATING

If, during Active Keto, you found that Window Eating helped you keep on top of when and what you ate, then it's a great idea to carry on with the schedule that you set up. Even if you can't keep to the 8 hour window (12pm to 8pm) every day, you could vary it so that you ate between 10am and 8pm, or even just made a firm rule to not eat after 8pm.

As this is a more relaxed (but always making informed decisions) way of eating, you don't need to always eat within the window. But you should aim to eat at least the majority of your days in this way. 4-6 days a week is perfect.

Carbs = Cardio

As any healthy plan is 80% food and 20% exercise, I've been focussing on what you eat throughout this book.

If you're a regular exerciser, I hope that you've found that, apart from during the first week, you've been able to exercise as normal while following the keto plan. You may, however, have noticed that you are lacking some strength and stamina. This is because it's harder to release energy from fats than carbs.

In this phase, we can start to use the carbs we eat to our advantage.

If you are planning on doing cardio exercise, you can tweak what you eat before and after you exercise. If you are exercising in the morning, you can have some carbs for your breakfast. I like to add a banana to my Nuts and Seeds Granola. After you've done some gruelling exercise, if you are feeling drained, you should also eat a carbohydrate-based meal or snack. If you listen to your body, now you are more in tune with it, you should go with what you fancy after exercising.

Finally, have you heard of carb loading? It's when, if you're doing a marathon or similar, you eat lots of carbs the night before. Now I'm not suggesting you do that! But if you do happen to have a big pizza one night, if you follow that with some intensive exercise the next morning, then you will have balanced it out. Good to know!

3 STRIKE RULE

One of the things that I have seen happen when people reach a more relaxed phase of any healthy eating plan, is that when you stop thinking so much about what you eat, you can find your bad habits creeping back up on you.

If you think you are at risk of this, then you should follow my 3 strikes rule. Basically, this means that every week you can have 3 small blips and no more.

A blip could be:
- *A big glass of wine (or cocktail or beer)*

- *A slice of cake or a couple of biscuits*
- *A meal out where you have bad carbs &/or sugar*
- *Snacking after 8pm*

For example, if you go out for a meal with friends and have a couple of drinks, then that would be all of your strikes for the week (one for the meal, two for the drinks)

If you have a slice of cake one day and one drink after work, then that would be two strikes.

Bad day at the office? Need a glass of wine? That's 1 strike.

Remember, if you eat a meal laden with carbs for dinner and you offset that with some serious exercise the next day then that doesn't count as a strike.

And if all else fails and you go completely over your 3-strike rule, then see below about how an OCCASIONAL blowout is allowed.

THE BLOWOUT

Here's why it's good for you!

A blowout is a time when you lose control of what you are eating and drinking. It may well involve one too many drinks. It leaves you with cravings and a hangover. You might feel bloated and run down for days afterwards.

Let's be realistic about this. We're trying to maintain a lifestyle where you eat less starchy carbs and next to no sweet carbs. A lifestyle is for the long-term. It's balanced, healthy and interesting. But if you follow this strictly for a long time, you'll find yourself turning down some of life's joys.

Do you find yourself:
- *Regularly turning down a night out?*
- *OR Not eating your own birthday cake?*
- *OR Not enjoying a free hotel breakfast buffet?*
- *OR Sober at a wedding?*

Then you have to consider whether your healthy eating goals have taken over your life and are cutting out some of the real joys of life?

That's right, I'm saying everyone should enjoy a blowout every now and then. And that means, pizza, wine, a packet of chocolate digestives or whatever takes your fancy!

I'm not saying every week, or even every month. But if you're going on holiday or are going to a wedding or party then go for it and enjoy yourself.

How to recover from a blowout

First things first, if your blowout involved considerable alcohol consumption then you need to allow for the fact that you'll probably eat carbs the day after the blowout as well. Your ability to resist carb cravings after eating lots of carbs AND drinking is doubly reduced because (a) you have eaten carbs and your body has switched back to using carbs as energy and (b) alcohol severely interferes with your sleep, meaning that you'll be exhausted with much higher cravings for sugary and salty foods.

For the day/night of the blowout AND for all of the next day you should not start your recovery. And even more importantly, you should not feel guilty about this. Concentrate on getting a really good night's sleep at the end of your rest day, ready to get back to normal the next day.

Over the next 3-5 days you are going to go active keto, cutting right back on carbs to make the transition back to burning fat for energy as quick and painless as possible.

On the first day, try to do some high intensity exercise (think sweaty exercise like running, HIT or dance). Cardio exercise is great for burning up all the remaining carbs in your system so you can start with a "clean slate". Also, you should take MCT oil if possible (about an hour before lunch is the perfect time) as this again will help the switch.

On the second & third days, you might feel lacking in energy. This is your body transitioning to the keto lifestyle. Don't exercise on these days, eat plenty of protein and healthy fats and keep up the MCT oil. This is like a milder version of "Keto flu" that you might have experienced when you first tried keto. You might also need a little more salt in your diet and/or a vitamin supplement.

On the fourth and fifth days you will start to feel a lot better. The bloated feeling from the carbs should have completely gone. Carry on with Active Keto until you feel you are back to where you were before the blowout, then return to eating healthy starchy carbs.

MY 3 FAVOURITE "GOOD CARB" MEALS

Everyday Dahl

Chicken Fajita Rice

Puy Lentil & Feta Salad

EVERYDAY DAHL

vegan / high protein / low fat

SERVES	TIME	CARBS	CALS
4	30M	45.4G	284

INGREDIENTS

250g (9oz) red lentils
600ml (3 cups) water
1 tbsp olive oil
4 black peppercorns
2 cloves
1 onion (or 1 cup frozen), peeled and chopped
1 heaped tsp garlic paste
1 heaped tsp ginger paste
0.5 tsp chilli powder
0.5 tsp turmeric
0.5 tsp ground coriander
1 tsp salt
1 x 400g (14oz) can chopped (crushed) tomatoes

Place the red lentils and water in a large saucepan and bring to the boil. Simmer on a medium heat for about 10-12 minutes, until the lentils have split. If there is a danger of the lentils sticking to the bottom of the pan, add a bit more water. Remove from the heat & drain.

Meanwhile, heat the olive oil in a deep lidded frying pan. Toss in the peppercorns and cloves and heat for a minute (or until you can smell them). Add the onions, stir through, and place the lid on the pan. Cook on the lowest heat for 10 minutes.

Remove the lid from the pan and stir in the garlic, ginger, spices and salt. Stir-fry for 2 minutes before adding the tinned tomatoes. Cook for 10 minutes with the lid off.

Stir the cooked lentils into the tomato mixture. Cook gently for a further 10 minutes. Add a little extra water while cooking if necessary.

NUTRITIONAL INFORMATION PER SERVING

Calories 284 | Fat 4.4g | Net carbs 45.4g | Protein 17.9g

CHICKEN FAJITA RICE

This all-in-one fajita dish is warming and comforting.

SERVES	TIME	CARBS	CALS
2	15M	47.6G	311

INGREDIENTS

1 tsp chilli powder
0.5 tsp cumin
1 tsp smoked paprika
0.5 tsp ground coriander
1 tsp salt
1 lime, juice of
1 tsp tomato paste

1 x 150g (5oz) chicken breast, cut into cubes
1 tsp olive oil
1 onion (or 1 cup frozen), peeled and chopped
1 green (bell) pepper, deseeded and chopped
half a cup basmati rice
scant 1 cup water

Place all the spices, salt, lime juice and tomato paste in a wide bowl and mix together. Add the chicken pieces and mix together thoroughly with your hands. Leave to stand for a few minutes while you prepare the rest of the meal.

Heat the olive oil in a lidded saucepan over a med-high heat. When hot, toss in the onion and sliced green pepper. Stir-fry for 1 minute before adding the chicken and marinade.

Add the rice to the pan and stir thoroughly so each grain of rice is coated in the marinade. Add the water and bring to simmering point. Stir once, then put the lid on the pan and turn the heat to low. Cook gently for 10 minutes.

Check that the chicken is cooked through and the rice is soft.

NUTRITIONAL INFORMATION PER SERVING

Calories 311 | Fat 4.4g | Net carbs 47.6g | Protein 15.5g

PUY LENTIL & FETA SALAD

A really balanced and filling meal.

SERVES	TIME	CARBS	CALS
2	2M	24.8G	404

INGREDIENTS

1 tsp sun dried tomato paste

2 tsp balsamic vinegar

 salt and freshly ground black pepper, to taste

200g (7.1oz) cooked puy lentils

6 peppadew piquante peppers, drained and quartered

80g (2.8oz) baby spinach leaves

60g (2.1oz) feta, crumbled

40g (1.4oz) walnut halves

In a bowl, mix together the sun-dried tomato paste, balsamic vinegar and salt and pepper.

Add the puy lentils and peppadew peppers. Mix well.

Layer up your salad in 2 bowls or containers.

Place the spinach leaves at the bottom and divide the lentil mixture between the two bowls. Crumble the feta over and finally top with the walnuts.

NUTRITIONAL INFORMATION PER SERVING

Calories 404 | Fat 23.1g | Net carbs 24.8g | Protein 20.5g

HOW TO USE THE RECIPES

All the recipes are designed to be simple and quick to make.

Each recipe shows the serving size, the cook time, cals per serving and most importantly the carbs per serving.

Remember when you are doing *Fire Up* or *Active Keto*, you are trying to keep your carbs below 40g each day.

You can follow one of the Meal Plans to keep you under this amount or you can mix and match. All the Meal Plans are designed to be under 30g carbs per day, to allow you a few extra carbs, like milk in a cup of tea (0.5g carbs), a handful of peanuts (1.7g carbs), or some homemade chocolate (1.2g carbs).

THE RECIPES

QUICK BREAKFAST

Chocolate Shake

Super Fruit Smoothie

Super Veg Smoothie

Almond & Flax Porridge

Nuts & Seeds Granola

Magnificent Muesli

CHOCOLATE SHAKE

vegan / high protein / low carb

SERVES	TIME	CARBS	CALS
1	5M	1.9G	205

INGREDIENTS

400ml almond milk
2 tbsp your favourite
protein powder

1 tsp cocoa powder
2 tsp erythritol
1 tsp psyllium husk
powder

Place the almond milk in a shaker or lidded jar. Add the rest of the ingredients. Shake well.

Leave for 2 minutes to thicken slightly. Shake again and enjoy.

NOTES

I have used whey protein powder here but you can use whichever you want.

NUTRITIONAL INFORMATION PER SERVING

Calories 205 | Fat 7.3g | Net carbs 1.9g | Protein 26.6g

SUPER FRUIT SMOOTHIE

vegan / high protein / low carb

SERVES	TIME	CARBS	CALS
1	**5M**	**3.9G**	**194**

INGREDIENTS

350ml (12.3oz) almond milk

handful frozen mixed berries

1 tbsp milled golden flaxseed

1 tbsp chia seeds

2 tsp erythritol

Pop everything in a blender and whizz up. Rest for 2 minutes to thicken slightly then serve.

NUTRITIONAL INFORMATION PER SERVING

Calories 194 | Fat 13.4g | Net carbs 3.9g | Protein 7.9g

SUPER VEG SMOOTHIE

vegan / high protein / low carb

SERVES	TIME	CARBS	CALS
1	**5 M**	**1.6 G**	**185**

INGREDIENTS

350ml (12 fl oz) almond milk

30g (1oz) baby spinach leaves

1 tbsp milled golden flaxseed

1 tbsp chia seeds

2 tsp erythritol

Pop everything in a blender and whizz up. Rest for 2 minutes to thicken slightly then serve.

NUTRITIONAL INFORMATION PER SERVING

Calories 185 | Fat 13.4g | Net carbs 1.6g | Protein 8.3g

ALMOND & FLAX PORRIDGE

vegan / high protein / low carb

SERVES	TIME	CARBS	CALS
1	2M	2.2G	232

INGREDIENTS

2 tbsp almond flour
1 tbsp milled golden
flaxseed

1 tsp chia seeds
half a cup almond milk

In a microwave-able bowl, stir the almond flour, flaxseeds
and chia seeds together. Pour over the milk and stir again.
Microwave for 90 seconds.

OPTIONAL TOPPINGS

1> 1 tsp cocoa + 2 tsp erythritol

2> 1/2 tsp cinnamon

3> 1 tbsp sugar free maple syrup

NUTRITIONAL INFORMATION PER SERVING

Calories 232 | Fat 13.9g | Net carbs 2.2g | Protein 18.1g

NUTS & SEEDS GRANOLA

vegetarian / high protein / low carb

SERVES	TIME	CARBS	CALS
12	**25M**	**3.3G**	**335**

INGREDIENTS

80g (2.8oz) macadamia nuts
80g (2.8oz) pecans
200g (7.1oz) chopped mixed nuts
40g (1.4oz) pumpkin seeds
40g (1.4oz) sunflower seeds
30g (1.1oz) chia seeds
60g (2.1oz) ground almonds
2 tbsp mild olive oil
50g (1.8oz) butter
50g (1.8oz) erythritol
half a tsp vanilla paste

Preheat the oven to 180C/160C fan. Roughly chop the macadamia and pecan nuts. You can do this by hand or by lightly pulsing in a food processor.

Place the macadamia, pecan and mixed chopped nuts in a large bowl and add the seeds and ground almonds. Stir.

In a small pan, heat the butter, mild olive oil, erythritol and vanilla paste together. Stir together until fully combined. Mix the melted butter into the granola mixture.

Spread over a baking tray and bake in the oven for 20 minutes, turning after 10 minutes, until lightly browned.

Cool completely on the baking tray, then transfer to an airtight container.

NOTES

The recipe makes 12 x 55g servings. Sub the butter for coconut oil to make the recipe vegan.

NUTRITIONAL INFORMATION PER SERVING

Calories 335 | Fat 30.8g | Net carbs 3.3g | Protein 9.1g

MAGNIFICENT MUESLI

vegan / low carb

SERVES	TIME	CARBS	CALS
8	**20M**	**2.7G**	**194**

INGREDIENTS

25g (0.9oz) macadamia nuts

25g (0.9oz) whole almonds

80g (2.8oz) flaked coconut

50g (1.8oz) sunflower seeds

25g (0.9oz) pumpkin seeds

20g (0.7oz) chia seeds

1 tbsp olive oil

1 a few drops vanilla extract

quarter of a tsp ground cinnamon

1 tbsp inulin

Pre-heat the oven to 180C/160C fan.

Roughly chop the macadamia nuts and almonds.

In a bowl, combine the nuts, coconut flakes, sunflower seeds, pumpkin seeds and chia seeds.

Whisk the vanilla and cinnamon into the olive oil and pour over the nuts and seeds. Stir thoroughly.

Arrange the muesli mix over a baking tray and bake in the oven for 15 minutes.

Allow to cool completely before mixing in the inulin.

NOTES

The granola makes 8 x 30g portions of muesli. Will keep for 2 weeks if stored in an airtight container.

Serve with almond milk and a little erythritol if desired.

NUTRITIONAL INFORMATION PER SERVING

Calories 194 | Fat 16.1g | Net carbs 2.7g | Protein 4.7g

WEEKEND
BREAKFAST

Big Veggie Breakfast

Perfect Pancakes 3 Ways

Smoked Salmon & Scrambled Eggs

Baked Egg with Ham

BIG VEGGIE BREAKFAST

Great weekend breakfast or brunch. Feels decadent but very healthy.

SERVES	TIME	CARBS	CALS
1	15M	4.7G	175

INGREDIENTS

6 cherry tomatoes, on the vine
1 large flat mushroom
half a tsp olive oil
1 tsp butter

3 oz baby spinach leaves
1 large egg, lightly poached
salt and freshly ground black pepper, to taste

Pre-heat the oven to 220C/200C fan/400F/Gas 7. Place the tomatoes and mushrooms on a small baking tray. Drizzle the olive oil over the mushroom. Roast in the oven for about 10 minutes.

Heat the butter gently in a lidded pan until melted. Add the spinach, put the lid on and cook for 1 minute. Immediately remove from heat and stir through. Transfer to a serving plate.

Arrange the mushrooms, tomatoes and poached egg over the spinach. Add a little salt and pepper to taste. Serve immediately.

NUTRITIONAL INFORMATION PER SERVING

Calories 175 | Fat 12.5g | Net carbs 4.7g | Protein 10.9g

PERFECT PANCAKES 3 WAYS

vegetarian / high protein / low carb

SERVES	TIME	CARBS	CALS
8	30M	0.8G	115

INGREDIENTS

1 cup cream cheese
3 large eggs, room
temperature
70g (2.5oz) almond flour

3 tbsp erythritol
70ml (2.5oz) almond milk
pinch of salt
1 tbsp olive oil

Place the cream cheese, eggs, almond flour, erythritol and almond milk in a blender and blend until smooth. You can also do this with a fork but it takes a while to get it really smooth. Leave the mixture to rest for 5 minutes. Put a dribble of olive oil in a heavy bottomed frying pan and wipe with a little kitchen paper. Repeat every other pancake.

Heat the pan on a med-high heat and when hot, put a ladle-full of batter in the pan. Immediately swirl the pan round so you get an even spread.

Leave to cook for a couple of minutes until the edges start to pull away from the pan. Then use a spatula to gently lift or toss the pancake. Cook the other side for a little less time and when lightly golden tip onto a plate. Repeat to make about 8-10 pancakes. Be warned the first one never comes out as planned - just like with regular pancakes!

The pancakes store pretty well in the fridge for several days, just store with sheets of greaseproof paper between.

OPTIONAL TOPPINGS

Sugar Free Jam / Easy Chocolate Sauce / Caramel Sauce

NUTRITIONAL INFORMATION PER SERVING

Calories 115 | Fat 8.6g | Net carbs 0.8g | Protein 7.8g

SMOKED SALMON & SCRAMBLED EGGS

SERVES	TIME	CARBS	CALS
1	**5M**	**2.5G**	**394**

INGREDIENTS

60g (2.1oz) smoked salmon
15g (0.5oz) butter
2 large eggs, room
temperature

1 tbsp almond milk
wedge of lemon, juice of
salt and freshly ground
black pepper, to taste

Arrange the smoked salmon on a plate.

Melt the butter in a small non-stick saucepan over a low heat.

Crack the egg into the pan and add the milk.

Heat the egg gently while stirring continuously. Remove from theheat while the eggs are scrambled but still soft and place on the plate with the salmon.

Squeeze the lemon juice over the salmon and season generously with salt and pepper. Serve immediately.

NUTRITIONAL INFORMATION PER SERVING

Calories 394 | Fat 29.9g | Net carbs 2.5g | Protein 24.1g

BAKED EGG WITH HAM

vegetarian / high protein / low carb

SERVES	TIME	CARBS	CALS
1	15M	3.1G	357

INGREDIENTS

half a leek, trimmed and
thinly sliced
1 tsp olive oil
1 slice of ham

1 large egg, lightly
whisked
2 slices tomato,
40g (1.4oz) cheddar
cheese, grated

Preheat the oven to 180C/160C fan/350F.

Place the leek and oil in a small microwaveable dish.
Cover with clingfilm (plastic wrap) and microwave on high
for 4 minutes. Leave to rest, still covered, for a further 2
minutes.

Place the leek at the bottom of a ramekin and top with the
ham.

Pour in the egg, then top with the tomato slices and
sprinkle with the cheese.

Bake in the oven for 10 minutes or until the egg is set and
the top is turning brown.

NUTRITIONAL INFORMATION PER SERVING

Calories 357 | Fat 25.5g | Net carbs 3.1g | Protein 26.7g

LUNCH
ON-THE-GO

Baked Goats Cheese Frittata

Protein Packed Tuna Salad

Prawn Salad

Greek Lunchbox Salad with Pine Nuts

Avocado, Egg & Cashew Nut Lunchbox

BAKED GOATS CHEESE FRITTATA

vegetarian / high protein / low carb

SERVES	TIME	CARBS	CALS
2	25M	5.8G	478

INGREDIENTS

1 tbsp olive oil
3 large eggs, room temperature
4 heaped tbsp natural greek yogurt
1 heaped tbsp cream cheese

1 spring (green) onion, trimmed and chopped
30g (1.1oz) sun-dried tomatoes in oil, cut into slices
100g (3.5oz) goats cheese, chopped or crumbled

Pre-heat the oven to 210C / 190C fan / 375F / Gas 7.
Take a 20cm / 8 in cake tin and wipe a little olive oil over the base and sides with kitchen paper.

Crack the eggs into a bowl and beat well. Add the greek yogurt, cream cheese and spring (green) onions and beat well with a fork. Arrange the sun-dried tomatoes and goats cheese in the cake tin, then pour the egg mixture over.

Bake in the oven for 18-20 minutes, or until the filling is just set and tinged with brown. Allow to cool slightly in the tin, before scraping a knife round the outside of the frittata and carefully removing from the tin. Cut into quarters.

NOTES
One serving is two quarters of the frittata.
It can be eaten warm with a green salad. Keeps for up to 2 days in the fridge. Easily wrapped in cling film for an on-the-go lunch.

NUTRITIONAL INFORMATION PER SERVING

Calories 478 | Fat 38.8g | Net carbs 5.8g | Protein 25.8g

PROTEIN PACKED TUNA SALAD

This is a great salad for taking to work in a lunchbox.

SERVES	TIME	CARBS	CALS
2	15M	5.2G	328

INGREDIENTS

2 large eggs, room
temperature
half a head broccoli florets
1 tsp olive oil
1 lemon, juice of
salt and freshly ground
black pepper, to taste

1 tsp Worcestershire sauce
1 x 160g (5oz) can tuna,
drained
1 avocado, de-stoned,
peeled and sliced
80g (3oz) baby spinach
leaves

Bring a small pan of water to the boil. Pierce the eggs and
drop gently into the water with a slotted spoon. Boil for
8-10 minutes then move immediately to cold water to cool.
Boil broccoli florets for 6-8 minutes - either separately or
in the same pan. Drain the broccoli and leave to cool.

Make the dressing by mixing the olive oil, Worcestershire
sauce and half the lemon juice together. Season with salt
and pepper. Combine with the drained tuna.

Toss the avocado in the remaining lemon juice. Arrange the
spinach, cooled broccoli and avocado over two plates or
meal prep containers. Add the seasoned tuna.

Finally, peel and halve the eggs and distribute between the
two dishes.

NUTRITIONAL INFORMATION PER SERVING

Calories 328 | Fat 20.8g | Net carbs 5.2g | Protein 30.2g

PRAWN SALAD

A very filling and satisfying salad.

SERVES	TIME	CARBS	CALS
1	10M	15.6G	473

INGREDIENTS

1 large egg, room temperature

1.5oz baby spinach leaves

5cm (2in) cucumber, halved lengthways and sliced

1 tomato, quartered

100g (3.5oz) frozen cooked and peeled king prawns (shrimp), thoroughly defrosted

15g (0.5oz) cashews

1 tbsp pumpkin seeds

1 tbsp sunflower seeds

25g (0.9oz) pomegranate seeds

1 tsp olive oil

1 tsp white wine vinegar

pinch of salt

Boil a small pan of water and boil the egg for 8 mins. Cool in cold water, then peel and half.

Arrange the spinach leaves, cucumber, tomato and prawns over a plate.

Sprinkle on the cashew nuts, pumkin seeds, sunflower seeds and pomegranate seeds.

In a small bowl, stir together the olive oil, white wine vinegar and pinch of salt. Pour over the salad and serve immediately.

NOTES

The salad can be stored in the fridge for a day. Keep the dressing separate and pour over just before serving.

NUTRITIONAL INFORMATION PER SERVING

Calories 473 | Fat 28.7g | Net carbs 15.6g | Protein 37.2g

GREEK LUNCHBOX SALAD
WITH PINE NUTS

SERVES	TIME	CARBS	CALS
1	5M	12.2G	538

INGREDIENTS

20g (0.7oz) pinenuts
80g (2.8oz) salad leaves
8 cherry tomatoes, halved
20g (0.7oz) sun-dried
tomatoes in oil
80g (2.8oz) feta, crumbled
1 tbsp simple vinaigrette
(page 190)

Heat a frying pan over a high heat. Add the pine nuts and cook, shaking the pan frequently, until they are lightly toasted. Remove from the pan to cool.

Place the salad leaves and cherry tomatoes in a bowl or lunchbox. Top with the sun dried tomatoes and feta.

Dress the salad with the vinaigrette (do this just before eating if this is a lunchbox) and finally sprinkle the pinenuts over the top.

NUTRITIONAL INFORMATION PER SERVING

Calories 538 | Fat 43.6g | Net carbs 12.2g | Protein 18.8g

AVOCADO, EGG & CASHEW NUT LUNCHBOX

SERVES	TIME	CARBS	CALS
1	15M	12.5G	405

INGREDIENTS

1 large egg, room temperature
80g (2.8oz) salad leaves
6 cherry tomato, halved
half a avocado, de-stoned, scooped from the skin and sliced

wedge of lemon, juice of
1 tbsp sweet & spicy sauce (page 192)
20g (0.7oz) cashews

Boil a small pan of water and boil the egg for 8 mins. Cool in cold water, then peel and half.

Arrange the salad leaves in a bowl or lunchbox and add the cherry tomatoes.

Add the avocado and squeeze over the lemon juice (this helps the avocado keep its colour).

Toss through the sweet and spice sauce (do this just before serving for a lunchbox) and top with the egg and cashew nuts.

NUTRITIONAL INFORMATION PER SERVING

Calories 405 | Fat 31.2g | Net carbs 12.5g | Protein 17.1g

MY TOP 3 TOAST TOPPERS

Creamy Mushrooms on Toast

Smashed Avocado & Poached Egg

Houmous Stuffed Pepper

CREAMY MUSHROOMS ON TOAST

This is a deliciously easy dinner for two.

SERVES	TIME	CARBS	CALS
2	15M	5.9G	176

INGREDIENTS

1 tsp olive oil
4 spring (green) onions, trimmed and chopped
250g (9oz) chestnut mushrooms, washed and sliced

1 tsp dried mixed herbs
1 tbsp soy sauce
scant 1 cup white wine
1 heaped tbsp cream cheese

Heat the oil in a lidded frying pan (skillet) on a med-high heat. Add the spring (green) onions and mushrooms and stir-fry for 2 minutes.

Add about 3 tbsp water, dried herbs, soy sauce and wine and cover. Cook for 5 minutes.

Take the lid off the pan, stir in the soft cheese and bubble gently for another minute.

NOTES

You can use any keto-friendly toast for this, but I love it on a 2-minute microwave roll.

NUTRITIONAL INFORMATION PER SERVING

Calories 176 | Fat 6.7g | Net carbs 5.9g | Protein 4.5g

SMASHED AVOCADO & POACHED EGG

SERVES	TIME	CARBS	CALS
1	5M	8.2G	426

INGREDIENTS

2 slices of golden flaxseed bread (page 55)

1 microwave poached egg (page 187)

half an avocado, stone removed, scooped out of the skin

6 cherry tomatoes, halved

half a tsp olive oil

1 tsp balsamic vinegar

Pop the golden flaxseed bread in the toaster. Make the microwave poached egg.

When the bread is toasted, place on a small plate.

Top with the avocado and lightly crush with a fork until creamy (but still with some chunks of avocado).

Add the tomatoes to the plate and drizzle over the olive oil and balsamic vinegar. Finally, place the egg on the top of the avocado. Season lightly with salt and pepper.

NUTRITIONAL INFORMATION PER SERVING

Calories 426 | Fat 30.0g | Net carbs 8.2g | Protein 27.1g

HOUMOUS STUFFED PEPPER

vegetarian / high protein / low carb

SERVES	TIME	CARBS	CALS
1	**20M**	**11.0G**	**362**

INGREDIENTS

half a red (bell) pepper, deseeded

1 tsp olive oil

2 slices of golden flaxseed bread (page 55)

40g (1.4oz) baby spinach leaves

2 tbsp houmous

pinch of paprika

Preheat the oven to 220C/200C fan.

Rub the olive oil over the red pepper half. Place on a baking tray. Bake in the oven for 15 minutes, turning once.

Toast the flaxseed bread and place on a plate. Add the spinach leaves.

Fill the red pepper with the houmous and place on the toast. Sprinkle a pinch of paprika over.

NUTRITIONAL INFORMATION PER SERVING

Calories 362 | Fat 23.9g | Net carbs 11.0g | Protein 19.0g

LUNCHTIME WARMERS

Lazy Carrot & Coriander

Creamy Tomato Soup

Detox Chicken Broth

Slow Onion Soup

LAZY CARROT & CORIANDER

vegan / low fat

. . . .

SERVES	TIME	CARBS	CALS
4	**30M**	**13.0G**	**64**

. . . .

INGREDIENTS

. . . .

half an onion (or 1/2 cup frozen), peeled and chopped

6 carrots (400g), peeled & roughly chopped

4 cups vegetable stock, fresh or made with 2 cubes

half a tsp garlic paste

1 tsp ground coriander

salt and freshly ground black pepper, to taste

Place the onions, carrots, vegetable stock, garlic paste and ground coriander in a slow cooker.

Cook on low for 8 hours or high for 4 hours.

Use a handheld blender to blitz the soup directly in the slow cooker dish (allow it to cool a bit first!)

Check the seasoning and add salt and pepper to taste.

Serve straight away or transfer to containers or bags to freeze.

NOTES

You can use frozen onion and carrot for this recipe, which means absolutely no chopping. Tastes so fresh, healthy and warming too!

You can also make this on the hob, by simmering the ingredients together for half an hour.

NUTRITIONAL INFORMATION PER SERVING

. . . .

Calories 64 | Fat 1.2g | Net carbs 13.0g | Protein 1.4g

CREAMY TOMATO SOUP

vegetarian / low carb

SERVES	TIME	CARBS	CALS
6	**20M**	**7.7G**	**134**

INGREDIENTS

1 tbsp olive oil
1 onion (or 1 cup frozen), peeled and chopped
1 tbsp tomato paste
0.5 heaped tsp garlic paste
2 x 400g (14oz) can chopped (crushed) tomatoes
400ml (14.1oz) water
1 tsp oregano (dried)
1 tsp salt
2 tsp balsamic vinegar
100ml (3.5oz) double cream

Heat the olive oil in a large saucepan. Add the onions and cook on a gentle heat for 5 minutes. Add the tomato paste and garlic and stir fry for 1 minute.

Add the chopped tomatoes and water and bring up to a simmer. Add the oregano, salt and balsamic vinegar. Simmer for 15 minutes.

Blend if you like the soup smooth (I leave it with chunks of tomato but that is personal preference - and laziness!)

Remove from the heat and stir in the cream.

NOTES

Great soup to freeze, then microwave for an easy lunch.

NUTRITIONAL INFORMATION PER SERVING

Calories 134 | Fat 10.3g | Net carbs 7.7g | Protein 2.0g

DETOX CHICKEN BROTH

high protein

SERVES	TIME	CARBS	CALS
4	2H	13.0G	126

INGREDIENTS

1 onion (flavour only) (or 1 cup frozen), peeled and chopped

1 carrot (flavour only), peeled and roughly chopped

2 celery stalks, trimmed and roughly chopped

8 black peppercorns

1 tsp salt

2 bay leaves

2 litres water

1 500g (1lb 2oz) chicken thighs or drumsticks

1 med/large parsnip

1 carrot, peeled and roughly chopped

1 med white potatoes, peeled and chopped

1 leek, trimmed and cut into rings

1 heaped tsp garlic paste

2 tbsp soy sauce

4 tsp English mustard

4 spring (green) onion, trimmed and chopped

0.5 tsp ground black pepper

Take a large lidded pan and place the onion, carrot and celery inside. Add the peppercorns, salt and bay leaf.

Pour in approximately 2 litres water and bring to a simmer. Place the lid on the pan and cook gently either on the hob or in a medium oven (170C fan) for 1½ hours. Add the chicken thighs or drumsticks for the last 30 minutes of cooking time.

Strain the broth through a sieve. Discard the vegetables and place the chicken drumsticks on a plate. Leave to cool for 15 minutes or until the drumsticks can be handled comfortably.

Return the broth to the pan. Add the parsnip, carrot, potato, leek and garlic to the broth and simmer for about

15 minutes until tender.

Remove the skin from the drumsticks and pull the chicken off the bone.

Discard the bones, skin and waste and separate the good chicken into 4 portions.

Add the soy sauce, English mustard and spring onions to the broth and stir. Add the pepper and taste to check the seasoning. Add the chicken back into the broth.

Serve immediately or divide between 4 bowls or containers.

NOTES

The broth can be kept chilled for 2 days or can be frozen. Reheat thoroughly before serving.

NUTRITIONAL INFORMATION PER SERVING
....
Calories 126 | Fat 3.2g | Net carbs 13.0g | Protein 9.8g

SLOW ONION SOUP

low carb

SERVES	TIME	CARBS	CALS
4	**2H**	**12.9G**	**230**

INGREDIENTS

2 tbsp olive oil
20g (0.7oz) butter
1lb 1oz onions, peeled and finely sliced
1 heaped tsp garlic paste
1 tsp dried thyme
2 bay leaf
salt and freshly ground black pepper, to taste
100ml (3.5oz) red wine
4 cups beef stock, fresh

Heat the olive oil and butter in a large lidded pan on a med-high heat. Stir in the onions and sizzle for a couple of minutes.

Add the garlic, thyme and bay leaf. Season generously with salt and pepper and stir.

Turn the heat to the lowest possible setting, put the lid on the pan and cook for about 1 hour, stirring occasionally. Add the wine and stock, then bring to a gentle simmer for 30 minutes.

NUTRITIONAL INFORMATION PER SERVING

Calories 230 | Fat 16.2g | Net carbs 12.9g | Protein 2.7g

15 MINUTE
DINNERS

Everyday Paneer Curry

Steak and Feta Salad

Pork & Shiitake Mushroom Stir Fry

Cauliflower Tofu Curry

Chinese Steak Salad

EVERYDAY PANEER CURRY

A simple vegetarian 'all-in-one' curry that tastes great.

SERVES	TIME	CARBS	CALS
2	15M	12.3G	313

INGREDIENTS

1 tbsp olive oil
half an onion (or half cup frozen), peeled and chopped
1 heaped tsp garlic paste
1 heaped tsp ginger paste
half a cup water
1 tsp cumin

0.5 tsp ground coriander
0.5 tsp turmeric
1 tsp salt
80g (2.8oz) spinach, fresh or frozen, chopped
2 tomatoes, roughly chopped
225g (7.9oz) paneer, cubed

Heat the oil in a wide lidded frying pan. Add the onions, garlic and ginger. Stir fry for 2 mins, then add the water and bring to a gentle simmer.

Add the salt plus the cumin, ground coriander and turmeric. Stir and cook with the lid on for 10 minutes.

Remove the lid from the pan. Add the spinach, tomatoes and paneer. Stir through. Cook with the lid on for 5-7 minutes.

NOTES

You can easily freeze leftovers from this meal.

NUTRITIONAL INFORMATION PER SERVING

Calories 313 | Fat 16.9g | Net carbs 12.3g | Protein 27.5g

STEAK AND FETA SALAD

This high protein and delicious salad is really quick to make.

SERVES	TIME	CARBS	CALS
2	10M	8.0G	394

INGREDIENTS

200g (7oz) sirloin steak
salt and freshly ground
black pepper, to taste
1 tbsp olive oil
1 tsp erythritol

2 tsp balsamic vinegar
3oz salad leaves
16 cherry tomatoes, halved
2oz feta, crumbled

Season the steaks well with salt and pepper and if possible leave it at room temp for a bit before cooking.

Heat a frying pan on a high heat and, when hot, add the steak to the pan. Cook for 1-3 minutes each side depending on thickness and how well cooked you like the steak. Remove to a plate, cover and leave to rest for 5-10 mins.

Prepare the dressing by mixing together the olive oil, erythritol and balsamic vinegar.

Arrange the salad leaves and cherry tomatoes over two serving plates. Divide the feta into two and crumble over both plates. Drizzle the dressing over.

Place the steaks on a chopping board and cut into thin slices with a sharp knife.

Arrange the sliced steak over both salads and enjoy!

NOTES

The key to making this delicious is to cook the steak first and to let it rest for 5 mins.

NUTRITIONAL INFORMATION PER SERVING

Calories 394 | Fat 25.2g | Net carbs 8.0g | Protein 34.8g

PORK & SHIITAKE MUSHROOM STIR FRY

SERVES	TIME	CARBS	CALS
2	**15M**	**13.7G**	**386**

INGREDIENTS

1 tbsp rapeseed oil
1 red onion, peeled and quartered
half a green (bell) pepper, deseeded and chopped
2 pork loin steaks (about 125g each), trimmed & cut into strips

120g (4.2oz) shiitake mushrooms, washed & quartered
250g (8.8oz) konjac noodles
2 tbsp sweet & spicy sauce (page 192)

Heat the rapeseed oil in a wok or large frying pan over a high heat. When hot, toss in the onion, peppers and pork strips. Cook for 4-6 minutes, until the pork is cooked through.

Remove the pork and veggies from the pan with a slotted spoon. Add the shiitake mushrooms and stir-fry for 3 minutes.

Meanwhile, rinse the noodles several times and dry on kitchen paper.

Add the noodles to the pan, stir-fry for a minute then put the vegetables and pork back in the pan. Reduce the heat, stir in the sauce and cook for a further 2 minutes.

NUTRITIONAL INFORMATION PER SERVING

Calories 386 | Fat 21.1g | Net carbs 13.7g | Protein 27.7g

CAULIFLOWER TOFU CURRY

My favourite way to eat cauliflower!

SERVES	TIME	CARBS	CALS
2	15M	10.9G	212

INGREDIENTS

150g (5.3oz) tofu, cut into cubes
1 tbsp olive oil
1 tsp cumin seeds
half a tsp mustard seeds
half a tsp nigella seeds
one medium cauliflower, cut into small florets
half a tsp cumin
quarter tsp turmeric
1 tsp ground coriander
half a tsp salt
1 lemon, juice of
2 tomatoes, finely chopped
5 tbsp water

Dry the tofu cubes on kitchen paper.

Heat the oil in the pan over a med-high heat. When hot, toss in the cumin, mustard and nigella seeds. Add the tofu and lightly fry for 2 minutes. Remove the tofu with a slotted spoon and set aside.

Add the cauliflower to the pan and fry for 2 minutes.

Meanwhile, mix the ground spices, salt and lemon juice in a small bowl.

Add the tomatoes, lemony spice mix and water to the pan, stir once, and put the lid on. Turn the heat to low and cook for about 10 minutes, or until the cauliflower is tender.

Add the tofu back to the curry and serve immediately.

NUTRITIONAL INFORMATION PER SERVING

Calories 212 | Fat 12.7g | Net carbs 10.9g | Protein 13.6g

CHINESE STEAK SALAD

I do love a good steak – and this one is VERY good!

SERVES	TIME	CARBS	CALS
2	**10M**	**9.8G**	**510**

INGREDIENTS

2 x 150g sirloin steak
1 tsp dried onion
1 tsp olive oil
0.5 heaped tsp ginger paste
3 tsp rice vinegar
1 tsp tomato ketchup
2 tsp water
1 tbsp olive oil
1 tbsp light soy sauce

100g (3.5oz) salad leaves
12 cherry tomatoes, halved
60g (2.1oz) beansprouts
half a carrot, peeled and grated
4 radishes, washed, trimmed and grated
1 tbsp sesame seeds

Heat a tsp olive oil in a frying pan until hot. Add in the steak, with a little seasoning of salt and pepper. Fry the steak for 3 minutes (or how you like it), turning once to give a medium rare steak that's a little pink in the middle.

When cooked remove the steak to a plate and leave to rest for 5 minutes.

In a small bowl, mix the dried onion, ginger, rice vinegar, tomato ketchup, water, olive oil and soy sauce. Rub a teaspoon of the dressing over the cooked steak.

Layer up the salad over two bowls. Add the salad leaves, cherry tomatoes, beansprouts, carrot and radishes. Pour the dressing over and gently mix.

Using a sharp knife, slice the beef thinly and divide between the salad bowls. Finally, scatter the sesame seeds over. Serve immediately.

NUTRITIONAL INFORMATION PER SERVING

Calories 510 | Fat 32.5g | Net carbs 9.8g | Protein 45.4g

SOUL FOOD, BOWL FOOD

Katsu Chicken Curry

Thai Fragrant Curry 3 ways

Thai Fragrant Curry Paste

Chicken Thai Curry

Prawn Thai Curry

Vegetarian Thai Fragrant Curry

Chilli Steak Ramen

Creamy Salmon & Leek Bowl

Slow-cooked Cambodian Chicken

Cod Ramen with Naked Noodles

KATSU CHICKEN CURRY

high protein / low carb

SERVES	TIME	CARBS	CALS
2	**20M**	**7.5G**	**463**

INGREDIENTS

2 x 150g (5oz) skinless and boneless chicken breast, cut into cubes

quarter of a 400g (14oz) can coconut milk

2 tbsp olive oil

1 heaped tsp garlic paste

1 heaped tsp ginger paste

2 tsp dried onion

0.5 tsp turmeric

2 tsp mild curry powder

2 tsp psyllium husk powder

1 cup chicken stock

pinch of salt

1 tsp light soy sauce

1 tsp erythritol

40g (1.4oz) baby spinach leaves

Place the cubed chicken in a bowl and stir in two tablespoons of coconut milk. Leave to marinate while you prepare the rest of the meal.

Heat 1 tbsp of the oil in a saucepan on a medium heat. Add the garlic and ginger and stir-fry for 2 minutes. Remove from the heat and stir in the dried onion, turmeric, curry powder and psyllium.

Return to the heat and add the chicken stock a little at a time, stirring continuously. Then add the coconut milk, soy sauce and sweetener. Bring up to a simmer, then turn the heat to low and continue to cook for a further 10 minutes. Stir in the spinach leaves just before you remove from the heat.

In a frying pan or griddle pan on a med-high setting, heat the remaining oil. When hot, add the chicken pieces in a single layer. Cook for 4-5 minutes each side until lightly charred and cooked through.

Layer up your plate or bowl with lightly cooked veggies (and rice for non-keto-ers). Place the chicken on top and pour over the sauce.

NOTES

A family favourite. I serve it for my kids with white rice. For myself, I serve it on a bed of lightly cooked veg.

As an added bonus the katsu sauce freezes really well so if you make a big batch you can have an easy chicken katsu every day of the week.

For vegetarians and vegans, just substitute the stock for vegetable stock and use tofu or seitan as your protein.

NUTRITIONAL INFORMATION PER SERVING

Calories 463 | Fat 26.9g | Net carbs 7.5g | Protein 28.8g

THAI FRAGRANT CURRY 3 WAYS

This is real soul food in a bowl. It's ready quickly and easily for a perfect weekday supper. The key is to make up a batch of Thai curry paste (it takes just a few minutes) and use only the amount you need in the curry. You can then freeze the paste – making your next one even quicker....

A choice of 3 – Prawn, Chicken or Vegetarian. Feel free to vary the vegetables depending on what you have spare. Note that vegetarians should replace the fish sauce with vegetarian oyster sauce.

THAI FRAGRANT CURRY PASTE

SERVES	TIME	CARBS	CALS
4	5M	5.0G	56

INGREDIENTS

1 tbsp olive oil
1 heaped tsp garlic paste
2 heaped tsp ginger paste
1 lime, zest only
1 tbsp chopped coriander stalks
1 tsp palm sugar (or brown sugar)
2 tsp lemongrass paste
2 tsp fish sauce (substitute with vegetarian oyster sauce if necessary)
quarter tsp cumin
quarter tsp turmeric
2 tsp vegetarian stock powder
1 tsp dried onion
pinch of salt

Place the oil in a small saucepan. Do NOT place on the heat. Add the garlic, ginger, lime zest, coriander stalks, palm sugar, lemongrass and salt.

Place on a medium heat and sizzle for about 2 minutes, stirring continuously. Remove from the heat. Stir in the cumin, turmeric, stock powder, dried onion and fish sauce.

Leave to cool. Use about a tbsp per person in the Thai currys. Freeze any that you have spare for next time.

NUTRITIONAL INFORMATION PER SERVING

Calories 56 | Fat 4.1g | Net carbs 5.0g | Protein 0.7g

serving.

CHICKEN THAI CURRY

high protein / low carb

SERVES	TIME	CARBS	CALS
2	**10M**	**18.8G**	**523**

INGREDIENTS

1 tbsp olive oil

2 x 150g (5oz) skinless and boneless chicken breast, cut into cubes

half a red onion, peeled and thinly sliced

2 spring (green) onion, trimmed and chopped

1 red (bell) pepper (or half cup mixed), deseeded and chopped

1 red chilli, de-seeded and cut into rings

2 portions thai fragrant curry paste (page 155)

half a 400g (14oz) can coconut milk

200ml (7.1oz) water

1 lime, juice of

handful fresh coriander (cilantro) leaves, chopped

Heat the oil in a saucepan on a medium heat. When hot, toss in the chicken, red onion, spring onion, peppers and chilli. Stir-fry for 2-3 minutes.

Add the curry paste and stir through. Add the coconut milk and water. Heat gently for 10 minutes.

Stir through the lime juice and coriander leaves just before serving.

NUTRITIONAL INFORMATION PER SERVING

Calories 523 | Fat 32.4g | Net carbs 18.8g | Protein 23.5g

PRAWN THAI CURRY

high protein / low carb

SERVES	TIME	CARBS	CALS
2	**10M**	**17.4G**	**452**

INGREDIENTS

1 tbsp olive oil

half a red onion, peeled and thinly sliced

2 spring (green) onion, trimmed and chopped

1 red (bell) pepper (or half cup mixed), deseeded and chopped

1 red chilli, de-seeded and cut into rings

2 portions thai fragrant curry paste (page 155)

half a 400g (14oz) can coconut milk

200ml (7.1oz) water

1 lime, juice of

250g (8.8oz) frozen cooked and peeled king prawns (shrimp)

handful fresh coriander (cilantro) leaves, chopped

Heat the oil in a saucepan on a medium heat. When hot, toss in the red onion, spring onion and peppers. Stir-fry for 2-3 minutes.

Add the curry paste and stir through. Add the coconut milk and water. Heat gently for 5 minutes.

Add the chillis and prawns. Add the lime juice. Heat for a further 5 minutes until the prawns are cooked. Stir in the coriander leaves just before serving.

NUTRITIONAL INFORMATION PER SERVING

Calories 452 | Fat 30.4g | Net carbs 17.4g | Protein 24.9g

VEGETARIAN THAI FRAGRANT CURRY

SERVES	TIME	CARBS	CALS
2	10M	22.1G	385

INGREDIENTS

1 tbsp olive oil

half a red onion, peeled and thinly sliced

2 spring (green) onion, trimmed and chopped

0.5 red (bell) pepper (or half cup mixed), deseeded and chopped

0.5 green (bell) pepper, deseeded and chopped

1 red chilli, de-seeded and cut into rings

100g (3.5oz) babycorn

100g (3.5oz) mange tout

2 portion thai fragrant curry paste (page 155)

half a 400g (14oz) can coconut milk

200ml (7.1oz) water

1 lime, juice of

handful fresh coriander (cilantro) leaves, chopped

Heat the oil in a saucepan on a medium heat. When hot, toss in the red onion, spring onion and peppers. Stir-fry for 2-3 minutes.

Add the curry paste and stir through. Add the coconut milk and water. Heat gently for 5 minutes.

Add the chillis, babycorn and mangetout. Add the lime juice. Heat for a further 5 minutes until the vegetables are tender. Stir in the coriander leaves just before serving.

NUTRITIONAL INFORMATION PER SERVING

Calories 385 | Fat 29.6g | Net carbs 22.1g | Protein 5.2g

CHILLI STEAK RAMEN

Warming, comforting and filling. Yum yum.

SERVES	TIME	CARBS	CALS
2	10M	10.6G	545

INGREDIENTS

300g (11oz) sirloin steak
 salt and freshly ground
black pepper, to taste
4 tbsp Hot Chilli Sauce
(page 191)
250g (9oz) konjac noodles
1 tbsp olive oil
600ml fresh beef stock

2 tbsp fish sauce
100g (3.5oz) beansprouts
2 spring (green) onions,
trimmed and chopped
handful fresh coriander
(cilantro) leaves, chopped
2 tbsp kimchee
2 wedges of lime

Heat a wok or wide frying pan to a high heat. Season the steak with salt and pepper and cook for 1-2 mins each side. The cooking time will vary depending on preference.

Place the steak(s) on a plate and spread half the hot chilli sauce over the steaks. Leave to rest for at least 5 minutes.

Rinse and drain the konjac noodles at least 3 times, then dry on kitchen paper.

Heat the olive oil in the wok on a med-high heat. Toss in the noodles and stir-fry for 3 minutes. Set aside.

Add the stock, fish sauce and the rest of the hot chilli sauce to the wok and bring up to a gentle simmer.

Add the beansprouts, spring onions and coriander to the pan and cook for a further 2 minutes.

Divide the noodles between 2 bowls and add the ramen. Slice the beef into thin slices and add to the bowls. Put a tablespoon of kimchee on the side and a wedge of lime.

NUTRITIONAL INFORMATION PER SERVING

Calories 545 | Fat 33.2g | Net carbs 10.6g | Protein 45.2g

CREAMY SALMON & LEEK BOWL

SERVES	TIME	CARBS	CALS
1	20M	15.0G	599

INGREDIENTS

1 heaped tsp butter
1 shallot, peeled and cut into slices
2 leeks, washed, trimmed and chopped into rings
1 salmon fillet
300ml vegetable stock, fresh or made with 1 cube
1 tsp fish sauce
2 tbsp creme fraiche
1 egg yolk
salt and freshly ground black pepper, to taste

Heat the butter in a wide lidded saucepan until it has melted. Stir in the shallot and leeks. Stir-fry for 2 minutes.

Place the salmon on top of the leeks and pour in the stock and fish sauce. Bring up to a simmer and cook with the lid on for 10 minutes. Remove from the heat (leaving the lid on) and rest for a further 5 minutes.

Whisk the creme fraiche and egg yolk together. Add a few tbsp of stock from the pan to the creme fraiche. Whisk again to loosen it.

Place the pan back on the heat and bring to a gentle simmer. Pour in the creme fraiche mixture and warm gently. Serve in a wide bowl with a good sprinkling of black pepper.

NUTRITIONAL INFORMATION PER SERVING

Calories 599 | Fat 42.3g | Net carbs 15.0g | Protein 29.7g

SLOW-COOKED CAMBODIAN CHICKEN

SERVES	TIME	CARBS	CALS
4	6 H	15.8G	442

INGREDIENTS

1 onion (or 1 cup frozen), peeled and chopped
1 red chilli, de-seeded and cut into rings
300g (10.6oz) chicken thighs, cut into pieces
half a tsp turmeric
half a tsp ground coriander
1 tsp dried onion
3 tbsp desiccated coconut
1 tsp galangal paste
1 tsp lemongrass paste
1 heaped tsp garlic paste

1 heaped tsp ginger paste
300ml (generous cup) coconut milk
1 tsp tamarind paste
1 green (bell) pepper, deseeded and chopped
200g (7.1oz) cauliflower, cut into florets
10 cherry tomatoes, halved
2 spring (green) onion, trimmed and chopped
a good handful fresh coriander (cilantro) leaves, chopped

Heat the oil in a large oven-proof saucepan (any saucepan if you are transferring to a slow cooker)

Add the onion and chilli. Stir in the chicken and cook until lightly browned.

Stir in the spices, onion and coconut. Then add the galangal, lemongrass, ginger and garlic pastes. Stir-fry for 2 minutes.

Add the coconut milk and tamarind paste. Bring up to a simmer. Now either transfer to a slow cooker for 6-8 hours or cook on a very low oven heat for about 6 hours.

Alternatively, cook in the oven at 160C fan for about 2 hours.

Add the green pepper, pak choi and cherry tomatoes and

cook gently for a further 20 minutes.

Divide the curry between two bowls and top with the spring onion and coriander.

NOTES

With a quick bit of prep early on, this is a great recipe for cooking slowly. You can leave it in the slow cooker all day.

NUTRITIONAL INFORMATION PER SERVING

Calories 442 | Fat 31.3g | Net carbs 15.8g | Protein 24.8g

COD RAMEN WITH NAKED NOODLES

SERVES	TIME	CARBS	CALS
2	**30M**	**12.0G**	**291**

INGREDIENTS

2 x 125g (4oz) cod fillet (skinless and boneless)
1 tsp oyster sauce
1 tbsp mirin
1 tbsp soy sauce
1 heaped tsp ginger paste
1 tsp toasted sesame oil
250g (8.8oz) konjac noodles
1 tbsp olive oil

200g (7.1oz) pak choi, washed, trimmed and divided into leaves
500ml (17.6oz) vegetable stock, fresh or made with 1 cube
2 tsp light soy sauce
1 tsp oyster sauce
1 tbsp fish sauce

Make a marinade for the cod by combining oyster sauce, mirin soy sauce, ginger and sesame oil. Rub the marinade all over the cod and leave to rest in the fridge for at least 10 minutes.

Meanwhile, prepare the noodles. Drain off the liquid in the packet and place in a big bowl or pan. Cover with cold water, stir and drain. Repeat as necessary. Then drain thoroughly and pat dry with kitchen paper.

Heat half of the olive oil in a frying pan or wok over a med-high heat. Fry the noodles for 2-3 minutes. Then remove from the pan and set aside. Fry the pak choi in the oil for a further 2 minutes, then add the vegetable stock, light soy sauce, oyster sauce and fish sauce. Simmer gently for 10 minutes.

Heat the remaining olive oil in a frying pan on a med-high heat. Add the marinated cod and cook for approx 10 minutes, turning once, until cooked through.

Layer up each ramen bowl with the noodles at the bottom, then the pak choi and stock and finally place the salmon on the top.

NOTES

I use "Naked" noodles, also called konjac or shiritaki noodles, for this dish. If you've tried them before and they weren't great, make sure you wash and dry them thoroughly and then dry fry for the best texture and taste.

NUTRITIONAL INFORMATION PER SERVING
....
Calories 291 | Fat 12.1g | Net carbs 12.0g | Protein 27.9g

FREEZER FILLERS

Healthy Fried Chicken

Fresh Chicken Curry

Best Beef Chilli

Chicken Korma

Mexican Pulled Pork

Aubergine, Spinach & Paneer Curry

HEALTHY FRIED CHICKEN

Once you've cooked 'fried' chicken like this you won't go back.

SERVES	TIME	CARBS	CALS
6	**30M**	**11.6G**	**223**

INGREDIENTS

half a cup buttermilk
0.25 tsp cayenne pepper
0.25 tsp paprika
4 x 150g (5oz) skinless and
boneless chicken breasts,
cut into 5-6 strips each

half a cup gram flour
salt and freshly ground
black pepper, to taste
0.5 tsp paprika
1 tbsp buttermilk
2 tbsp olive oil

Mix the buttermilk with the cayenne pepper and paprika.
Add the chicken strips and smush it around with your
hands to ensure the chicken is evenly coated with
buttermilk. Refrigerate overnight or at least 4 hours.

When you are ready to cook the chicken, mix the gram
flour, salt and pepper, paprika, baking powder and 1
tbsp buttermilk in a large bowl. It should be a bit like
breadcrumbs.

Preheat the oven to 220C/200C fan/425F/Gas Mark 7. Press
the chicken pieces firmly into the flour and toss. Set the
breaded chicken on a plate.

Heat the olive oil in a large wide frying pan on a med-high
heat. Place a few chicken pieces in the oil, leaving a bit of
space between them. Cook for 2 minutes each side, then
transfer to a baking tray. Repeat until all the chicken has
been fried. Bake in the oven for 8 minutes.

NOTES

My kids absolutely love this! The chicken is baked in a hot oven after flash frying.

You can freeze the chicken pieces after the frying process and then bake from frozen.

After the frying step, transfer to a plate and allow to cool completely. Freeze. Cook from frozen in the oven set to 220C/200C fan/425F/Gas Mark 7 for 16-18 minutes.

NUTRITIONAL INFORMATION PER SERVING
....
Calories 223 | Fat 7.2g | Net carbs 11.6g | Protein 18.6g

FRESH CHICKEN CURRY

This is my absolute favourite chicken curry recipe. It's so so simple.

SERVES	TIME	CARBS	CALS
2	30M	14.9G	222

INGREDIENTS

1 onion (or 1 cup frozen), peeled and chopped

1 heaped tsp garlic paste

1 tsp chilli powder

1 tbsp olive oil

0.5 tsp ground coriander

0.5 tsp cumin

1 tsp salt, or to taste

2 green chillies, de-seeded and cut into rings

4 tomatoes, roughly chopped

4 tbsp water

1 handful fresh coriander (cilantro) leaves, chopped (optional)

1 x 150g (5oz) skinless and boneless chicken breasts, cut into cubes

Heat the oil in a large lidded saucepan over a very low heat. Add the onion, garlic and ginger pastes and chillies. Cook on low with the lid on for 10 minutes.

Add the tomatoes, water, spices, black pepper, salt and fresh coriander (if using). Cook on a low heat with the lid on for a further 10 minutes.

Add the chicken breast, bring to a simmer and cook for a further 12 minutes or until the chicken is tender.

NOTES

This curry can be frozen in individual portions and cooked from frozen.

NUTRITIONAL INFORMATION PER SERVING

Calories 222 | Fat 9.1g | Net carbs 14.9g | Protein 13.5g

BEST BEEF CHILLI

This is a keeper. A true bung-it-all-in chilli.

SERVES	TIME	CARBS	CALS
4	2H	11.4G	271

INGREDIENTS

500g (1lb 2oz) minced (ground) beef 5% fat

1 onion (or 1 cup frozen), peeled and chopped

1 red (bell) pepper (or half cup mixed), deseeded and chopped

1 heaped tsp garlic paste

1 tsp salt

1 tsp paprika

1 tsp chilli powder

1 tsp cumin

1 lime, juice of

half a tsp black pepper

1 tsp chilli (red pepper) flakes

1 tsp cocoa powder (unsweetened)

1 x 400g (14oz) can chopped (crushed) tomatoes

1 x 400g (14oz) can kidney beans, pour it all in, water and all

Break up the minced beef with your hands and arrange over the bottom of a casserole dish or slow cooker.

Add all the ingredients except the lime juice.

Cook in your slow cooker on low for 8 hours or high for 4 hours. Alternatively, cook in the oven at 160C/140C fan/325F/Gas Mark 3 for 2 hours. Add the lime juice after cooking.

NOTES

The chilli can be kept in the fridge for 24 hours or frozen. You'll find that the flavour actually improves with time.

NUTRITIONAL INFORMATION PER SERVING

Calories 271 | Fat 6.4g | Net carbs 11.4g | Protein 40.9g

CHICKEN KORMA

A lovely, healthy way to make a family-friendly curry from scratch.

SERVES	TIME	CARBS	CALS
4	**15M**	**10.4G**	**365**

INGREDIENTS

1 heaped tsp coconut oil
1 onion (or 1 cup frozen), peeled and chopped
1 heaped tsp garlic paste
1 heaped tsp ginger paste
3 tbsp tomato paste
1 tsp salt
0.5 tsp turmeric
0.5 tsp ground coriander

0.5 tsp paprika
0.5 tsp cumin
0.5 tsp chilli powder
0.5 tsp dried fenugreek leaves
3 x 150g (5oz) skinless and boneless chicken breasts, cut into cubes
1 x 400g (14oz) can coconut milk

Heat the coconut oil over a high heat until melted. Add the onions, garlic, ginger, tomato paste, salt and all the spices. Stir fry for 1 minute. Add the chicken and continue to stir fry for a further 2 minutes.

Pour in the coconut milk, stir, put the lid on the pan and cook for 8 minutes.

Remove the lid and cook, lid off, for a further 2-4 minutes.

NOTES

The key ingredient is dried fenugreek leaves. If your supermarket doesn't stock them then a good health food shop or Indian store will definitely have them.

Chicken korma can be frozen in individual portions and re-heated from frozen.

NUTRITIONAL INFORMATION PER SERVING

Calories 365 | Fat 23.3g | Net carbs 10.4g | Protein 17.1g

MEXICAN PULLED PORK

Great cooked slowly in the oven or in your slow cooker.

SERVES	TIME	CARBS	CALS
6	**3H**	**9.6G**	**550**

INGREDIENTS

1 pork shoulder joint (approx 1.2kg)
salt and black pepper
2 red onions, quartered
6 tbsp chipotle sauce (page 193)
4 heaped tsp garlic paste
1 tsp salt
1 tsp ground coriander
1 tsp cumin
1 tsp oregano (dried)
1 cup water
2 bay leaves
2 handfuls fresh coriander (cilantro) leaves, chopped
2 limes, juice of

Pre-heat the oven to 160C/140C fan/325F/Gas Mark 3. Place the shoulder joint in a large lidded casserole dish (or the base of your slow cooker). Season well with salt and pepper. Arrange the red onions around the pork.

In a bowl, combine the chipotle sauce, garlic, salt and all the herbs and spices. Add the water, stir in, then pour over the pork. Push the bay leaves into the sauce.

Cook in the oven (lid on) for approximately 3 hours. Or cook in your slow cooker for a minimum of 8 hours.

Remove from the oven and cut off and remove excess fat. Use 2 forks to pull the pork apart and stir into the sauce. Stir in the lime juice and fresh coriander.

NOTES
Serve in a tortilla wrap. Optional extras: salsa, guacamole, sour cream and grated cheese. You can freeze the cooked pork in convenient sized portions and reheat from frozen.

NUTRITIONAL INFORMATION PER SERVING

Calories 550 | Fat 34.5g | Net carbs 9.6g | Protein 49.4g

AUBERGINE, SPINACH & PANEER CURRY

SERVES	TIME	CARBS	CALS
4	**30M**	**13.6G**	**327**

INGREDIENTS

250g (8.8oz) paneer, cut into cubes

0.5 tsp turmeric

1 tsp chilli flakes

1 tsp salt

2 red onions, peeled and quartered

1 large aubergine, washed, quartered and cut into slices

2 tbsp olive oil

1 heaped tsp garlic paste

1 heaped tsp ginger paste

2 curry leaves

2 heaped tsp garam massala

0.5 tsp cumin

0.5 tsp freshly ground black pepper

200ml (7.1oz) water

half a can coconut milk

150g (5.3oz) baby spinach leaves

handful fresh coriander (cilantro) leaves, chopped (optional)

Preheat the oven to 220C/200C Fan.

Pat dry the paneer with kitchen paper. Sprinkle the turmeric, chilli flakes and salt over the paneer and toss through to make sure the paneer is well-coated. Leave to rest for 5 minutes.

Arrange the paneer, red onion and aubergine over a large baking tray. Drizzle over 1 tbsp of the olive oil. Cook in the oven for 20 minutes.

Heat the remaining olive oil in a large saucepan on a medium heat. Add the garlic and ginger pastes, curry leaves, spices and black pepper and stir-fry for one minute before adding the water and coconut milk. Simmer gently for ten minutes.

Add the roasted paneer and veg to the sauce and cook for a further 5 minutes. Finally, add the spinach and coriander leaves and allow to wilt into the sauce.

NOTES

Warming but not too spicy. This dish is my other half's favourite for a quick tea when he's home alone.

Great fresh or frozen. Make a big batch and freeze in smaller portions. Can be cooked straight from frozen in the microwave.

NUTRITIONAL INFORMATION PER SERVING
....
Calories 327 | Fat 21.6g | Net carbs 13.6g | Protein 17.0g

DESSERTS AND TREATS

Cookie Dough Rocks

Individual 2 min Cheesecakes

Vanilla Yogurt

Goo-ey Chocolate Brownie Mug Mix

Easy Chocolate Sauce

Individual Chocolate Puds

Caramel Sauce

COOKIE DOUGH ROCKS

vegan / high protein / low carb

SERVES	TIME	CARBS	CALS
15	5M	1.8G	73

INGREDIENTS

50g (1.8oz) cocoa powder
100g (3.5oz) erythritol, powdered

150g (5.3oz) peanut butter (no added sugar)

a few drops vanilla extract

Mix the cocoa powder and erythritol together in a small bowl until fully combined. Remove about a quarter of the mix to a plate.

Add the peanut butter and vanilla to the bowl. Mix together until you get a soft squidgy dough.

Take pinches of the dough (each rock should be about the size of a grape) and roll it in your hands to make a "rock". Then roll it in the cocoa and erythritol powder so it is fully covered. Repeat with the rest of the dough. The mix makes 20-30 rocks.

NOTES

Sometimes you just want a simple sweet chocolate-y hit. And these cookie dough rocks press all my buttons.

Ready to eat and can be stored in the fridge for several days.

These rocks are incredibly rich. A portion is 1-2 rocks depending on size.

NUTRITIONAL INFORMATION PER SERVING

Calories 73 | Fat 5.9g | Net carbs 1.8g | Protein 3.4g

INDIVIDUAL 2 MIN CHEESECAKES

SERVES	TIME	CARBS	CALS
1	2M	5.8G	221

INGREDIENTS

2 heaped tbsp natural greek yogurt
1 tsp vanilla paste
1 tsp erythritol

1 heaped tbsp Nut & Seed Granola (page 113)
1 tbsp Sugar Free Jam (page 189)

Using a fork, blend together the Greek yogurt, vanilla and erythritol until smooth.

In a ramekin or small dish, layer up the cheesecake. Press the granola into the bottom of the dish, add the yogurt mix and swirl the jam over the top.

NUTRITIONAL INFORMATION PER SERVING

Calories 221 | Fat 16.5g | Net carbs 5.8g | Protein 9.7g

VANILLA YOGURT

Just a really simple way to let delicious yogurt into your life!

SERVES	TIME	CARBS	CALS
1	1M	4.0G	101

INGREDIENTS

100g (3.5oz) natural greek yogurt

1 tbsp water
1 tsp vanilla paste
1 tsp erythritol

Place all the ingredients in a small bowl and mix well.

NUTRITIONAL INFORMATION PER SERVING

Calories 101 | Fat 5.0g | Net carbs 4.0g | Protein 9.0g

GOO-EY CHOCOLATE
BROWNIE MUG MIX

SERVES	TIME	CARBS	CALS
1	2M	3.2G	295

INGREDIENTS

1 heaped tsp butter
1 tbsp cocoa powder
(unsweetened)
1 tbsp erythritol

half a tsp vanilla paste
2 tsp coconut flour
half a tsp baking powder
2 tbsp double cream

Heat the butter in a mug or ramekin for 20 seconds until melted.

Stir in the other ingredients really well. Microwave for 1 minute. The brownie should have risen at the edges but still be melty in the middle.

NUTRITIONAL INFORMATION PER SERVING

Calories 295 | Fat 26.3g | Net carbs 3.2g | Protein 5.0g

EASY CHOCOLATE SAUCE

Very quick and easy (and rather decadent too!)

SERVES	TIME	CARBS	CALS
4	2M	0.9G	87

INGREDIENTS

30g (1.1oz) butter
20g (0.7oz) cocoa mass
2 tbsp erythritol

1 tsp vanilla paste
1 tbsp almond milk

Pop all the ingredients in a small microwave-able bowl.

Microwave for 30 seconds. Stir and rest. Give it another 10 second blast if needed.

NOTES

You can sub the cocoa mass for a tbsp of cocoa powder if needed.

NUTRITIONAL INFORMATION PER SERVING

Calories 87 | Fat 8.8g | Net carbs 0.9g | Protein 0.8g

INDIVIDUAL CHOCOLATE PUDS

SERVES	TIME	CARBS	CALS
1	2M	4.2G	447

INGREDIENTS

1 heaped tsp butter
3 tbsp almond flour
1 tsp cocoa powder
(unsweetened)
half a tsp baking powder

pinch of salt
half a tsp vanilla paste
1 large egg, room
temperature
1 tbsp chocolate sauce
(page 181)

Place the butter in a small bowl or ramekin. Microwave for 20 seconds to melt the butter.

Add flour, cocoa powder, baking powder, pinch of salt, vanilla, egg and water.

Use a fork to stir and whisk the ingredients together until you have a smooth batter. Rest for a minute to thicken slightly.

Microwave for 1 min 30 secs. Run a knife around the edge and flip the roll onto a small plate. Tip the chocolate sauce over.

NUTRITIONAL INFORMATION PER SERVING

Calories 447 | Fat 31.6g | Net carbs 4.2g | Protein 30.3g

CARAMEL SAUCE

vegetarian / low carb

. . . .

SERVES	TIME	CARBS	CALS
2	**2M**	**0.8G**	**126**

. . . .

INGREDIENTS

. . . .

30g (1.1oz) butter
1 tsp Monin Caramel   1 tbsp inulin
Sugar-free Syrup

Pop all the ingredients in a small microwave-able bowl.

Microwave for 20-30 seconds. Stir well.

NUTRITIONAL INFORMATION PER SERVING

. . . .

Calories 126 | Fat 12.2g | Net carbs 0.8g | Protein 0.1g

MISCELLANEOUS

Microwave Poached Egg

Cauliflower Pickle

Sugar Free Jam

Simple Vinaigrette

Hot Chilli Sauce

Sweet & Spicy Sauce

Chipotle Sauce

MICROWAVE POACHED EGG

SERVES	TIME	CARBS	CALS
1	2M	0G	85

INGREDIENTS

1 large egg, room temperature

1 tsp white wine vinegar
half a cup water, boiling

Take a small bowl, cup or ramekin and add the vinegar and water. Use a spoon to swirl the water in the cup.

With the water still swirling, break the egg on the side of the cup and lower into the water.

Microwave for 30 seconds. Leave to rest in the water for 2 minutes.

Scoop out from the water with a spoon and serve immediately.

NOTES

This is a fantastically simple idea which brings poached eggs within the realms of a quick breakfast. Learn this simple technique and you won't look back.

NUTRITIONAL INFORMATION PER SERVING

Calories 85 | Fat 5.7g | Net carbs 0.0g | Protein 8.3g

CAULIFLOWER PICKLE

Delicious with strong, salty cheese.

SERVES	TIME	CARBS	CALS
12	20M	1.4G	32

INGREDIENTS

1 medium cauliflower, cut into small florets
1 tbsp olive oil
1 tsp cumin seeds
1 heaped tsp garlic paste
1 cup white wine vinegar
100g (3.5oz) erythritol
2 tbsp chia seeds
1 tsp salt
1 tsp turmeric
2 cloves
2 bay leaves

Pre-heat the oven to 220C/200C fan.

Cut the cauliflower into very small florets and place in a large bowl.

In a small bowl, whisk together the olive oil, cumin seeds and garlic paste. Pour over the cauliflower and mix together with your hands. Transfer to a baking tray and cook for 15 minutes.

Meanwhile, heat the white wine vinegar in a small pan until steaming. Stir in the erythritol a tbsp at a time.

Add the chia seeds to the vinegar, along with the salt and turmeric.

Arrange the cauliflower between 2 clean jam jars. Add a clove and a bay leaf to each jar.

Pour the hot vinegar into each jar equally and lightly press the cauliflower into the vinegar.

Place the lid on the jars and leave to cool. Leave for 2 weeks before using.

NUTRITIONAL INFORMATION PER SERVING

Calories 32 | Fat 1.9g | Net carbs 1.4g | Protein 1.1g

SUGAR FREE JAM

vegan / high protein

. . . .

SERVES	TIME	CARBS	CALS
12	**5M**	**1.5G**	**17**

. . . .

INGREDIENTS

. . . .

250g (8.8oz) frozen mixed berries
2 tbsp chia seeds

2 tbsp erythritol
half a cup boiling water

Place the berries in a large microwave-safe bowl. Add the chia seeds and erythritol.

Pour the boiling water over and stir.

Microwave for 2 minutes. Stir. Microwave for a further minute.

Check the sweetness and add a bit more erythritol if desired.

Transfer to a lidded jar while still hot (the jam will thicken further as it cools) and refrigerate once cool.

Notes

I use Sainsburys Mixed Summer Berries (frozen) for this recipe, but you could go for just strawberries, raspberries etc or any combination.

The recipe makes approximately 12 generous 1 tbsp servings.

NUTRITIONAL INFORMATION PER SERVING

. . . .

Calories 17 | Fat 0.7g | Net carbs 1.5g | Protein 0.7g

SIMPLE VINAIGRETTE

vegan / low carb

SERVES	TIME	CARBS	CALS
6	**2M**	**0.3G**	**64**

INGREDIENTS

3 tbsp olive oil
2 tbsp white wine vinegar
1 tsp balsamic vinegar

1 tsp English mustard
1 tsp erythritol
salt and freshly ground black pepper, to taste

In a small bowl, stir together all the ingredients. Season generously with salt and pepper.

Transfer to a lidded jar or bottle.

NOTES

Makes 6 x 1 tbsp servings. Can be stored in a lidded container for 2 weeks.

NUTRITIONAL INFORMATION PER SERVING

Calories 64 | Fat 7.0g | Net carbs 0.3g | Protein 0.1g

HOT CHILLI SAUCE

Great for jazzing up red meat

SERVES	TIME	CARBS	CALS
4	**5M**	**2.2G**	**13**

INGREDIENTS

1 tbsp sriracha hot sauce
1 tbsp tomato paste
2 tsp erythritol

1 heaped tsp garlic paste
1 tsp paprika
2 tbsp white wine vinegar

Simply mix all the ingredients in a small bowl or cup.

NOTES

Great for jazzing up red meat (or anything really). Feel free to up the sriracha if you like it hot!

Use immediately or store in a lidded jar in the fridge for up to 2 weeks.

NUTRITIONAL INFORMATION PER SERVING

Calories 13 | Fat 0.2g | Net carbs 2.2g | Protein 0.4g

SWEET & SPICY SAUCE

vegan / low carb

SERVES	TIME	CARBS	CALS
4	2M	2.4G	47

INGREDIENTS

2 tsp dried onion
1 heaped tsp ginger paste
2 tbsp rice vinegar
2 tsp tomato ketchup

1 tsp tomato paste
2 tbsp water
1 tbsp olive oil
2 tbsp light soy sauce

In a small bowl, mix the dried onion, ginger, rice vinegar, tomato ketchup, tomato paste, water, olive oil and soy sauce.

NOTES

Store in a lidded jar in the fridge for up to 2 weeks.

NUTRITIONAL INFORMATION PER SERVING

Calories 47 | Fat 3.6g | Net carbs 2.4g | Protein 0.1g

CHIPOTLE SAUCE

Make any meal Mexican with this Chipotle Sauce.

SERVES	TIME	CARBS	CALS
6	**5 M**	**1.2 G**	**27**

INGREDIENTS

1 tbsp olive oil
1 heaped tsp garlic paste
1 tbsp tomato paste
2 tsp chipotle flakes
1 tbsp erythritol

2 tsp dried onion
half a tsp smoked paprika
half a tsp cumin
1 tbsp white wine vinegar
2 tbsp water

Heat the olive oil in a small pan on a low heat. Add the garlic and tomato pastes. Sizzle for 1 minute then remove from the heat.

Add the chipotle flakes, erythritol, onion and spices, then stir through.

Add the vinegar and water.

NOTES

The recipe makes 6 servings of 1 tbsp. If you don't use it all immediately, the sauce will keep in the fridge in a lidded jar for about 2 weeks.

NUTRITIONAL INFORMATION PER SERVING

Calories 27 | Fat 2.4g | Net carbs 1.2g | Protein 0.2g

Printed in Poland
by Amazon Fulfillment
Poland Sp. z o.o., Wrocław

52487096R00115